Child Killer

The True Story of The Atlanta Child Murders

Jack Rosewood

ISBN: 9781731400192

Copyright © 2018 by LAK Publishing

ALL RIGHTS RESERVED

No part of this book may be reproduced, stored in a retrieval system, or transmitted in any form or by any means, electronic, mechanical, photocopying, recording, scanning, or otherwise, without the prior written permission of the publisher.

FREE BONUS!

Get two free books when you sign
up to my VIP newsletter at
http://www.jackrosewood.com/free
150 interesting trivia about serial killers and
the story of serial killer Herbert Mullin.

Contents

Introduction 1

CHAPTER 1: The Killings Begin **7**

   Edward Smith and Alfred Evans 9

   Milton Harvey and Yusef Bell 12

CHAPTER 2: Wayne Bertram Williams **17**

   Early Life 18

   The Talent Agent 22

   Gemini 25

   The Night Owl 27

   The Fantasy World of Wayne Williams 29

CHAPTER 3: More Murders **34**

   Getting Sloppy 36

   How Were there So Many? 39

CHAPTER 4: Heightened Alert **42**

   Expanding His Territory 43

   STOP 46

   The Task Force Is Created 47

CHAPTER 5: No End in Sight 53

    Saturday Searches 55

    One Victim a Week 58

    "He Got in the Car" 61

    More Public Outcry..64

CHAPTER 6: The Pressure Builds 66

    A Change in M.O. 67

    The Bloody Chattahoochee 69

    The Stakeout..72

    Wayne Williams VS the Task Force 77

    Cleaning Up 80

    The Developing Case Against Wayne Williams 83

    The Press Conference 88

    Cat and Mouse 92

CHAPTER 7: The Trial of Wayne Williams 96

    The Arrest 97

    The Prosecution's Case 101

    The Defense 112

    The Verdict 118

CHAPTER 8: Unresolved Issues...120

    A Public Cause 121

    New Hope for Wayne Williams 124

    A Red Herring 127

    Other Possible Killers 133

    Accomplices? 138

    Other Conspiracies? 140

    Opportunists? 145

CHAPTER 9: New Revelations 147

    A New Investigation 148

    Back to Normal 151

    Wayne Williams in Prison 153

    New DNA Testing..158

    The Atlanta Child Murders in Popular Media 161

CHAPTER 10: Some Other Notable Black Serial Killers 167

    Jake Bird (1901-1949) 168

    Carl "Coral" Eugene Watts (1953-2007) 169

    Lorenzo Gilyard 171

    Harrison Graham 172

    The "Grim Sleeper" Lonnie David Franklin Junior 174

    The "Southside Slayer" Chester Dewayne Turner...................175

    Maury Travis (1965-2002), the Videotape Killer 177

    Wayne Williams Takes His Place among His Peers 178

Conclusion 180

A Note From The Author 189

Introduction

From July 1979 until May 1981, the city of Atlanta, Georgia was subjected to a state of terror by a relentless and sadistic serial killer who preyed primarily on black boys and young black men. By the time the reign was over, twenty-eight children and young adults were dead. Americans in general were shocked, and the people of Atlanta were traumatized.

Atlantans were used to a certain amount of crime, but not of the magnitude or type they had experienced during that period.

The case became officially known by law enforcement and legal experts as the "Atlanta Murders of 1979-1981," but was referred to more colloquially as the "Atlanta Child Murders" , due to twenty-two of the victims being under the age of eighteen. By the time the case was over, it had proved to be like none other in American history.

One of the most intriguing, and at the time terrifying aspects of the Atlanta Child Murders was that it took place in "real time." In most cases, it is not revealed that an offender is a serial killer until after he or she has been captured – law enforcement often don't even know that they have a serial killer on their hands.

This was not the case with the Atlanta Child Murders.

After the first few cases, the local media began to report on the abnormally high number of black boys who were missing in Atlanta. When their bodies started turning up in vacant lots and wooded areas, national media outlets picked up the case, placing extreme pressure on local law enforcement.

The enhanced media scrutiny also led to mobilization by members of the black community, who believed that they were not adequately served by law enforcement since all of the victims were black, which was no doubt partially the result of Atlanta being a symbol of the "Old South". Atlanta definitely had a recent history that was associated with segregation and organizations such as the Ku Klux Klan, but by the time of the murders it also had a black mayor and a majority black city council.

In other words, the racial dynamics surrounding the case were complex at times.

As the Atlanta serial murders progressed and politics entered into the equation, a task force was created to catch the killer. The FBI gave assistance to the GBI (Georgia Bureau of Investigation) as well as Atlanta, Fulton County, and Dekalb County law enforcement agencies. With over 100 agents working fulltime on the task force, it was only a matter of time until the serial killer was captured.

And when Wayne Williams finally was arrested, many people were surprised.

When the first media reports began to surface with Wayne Williams' name and picture in June 1981, he looked far from what most think of as a serial killer. The slightly overweight, glasses-wearing twenty-three-year-old Williams looked more like a computer nerd than a serial killer.

And he was black.

In 1981, the term "serial killer" was only seven-years-old, first being coined by legendary FBI profiler Robert Ressler in 1974, and few had heard it used. Those who were familiar with the term thought of most serial killers as middle-aged white males.

Wayne Williams' arrest and later conviction for two of the Atlanta murders challenged many people's assumptions about serial killers.

According to the Radford University Database, which is one of the most comprehensive database of serial killer demographics, about sixty-seven percent of all American serial killers are white, while twenty-five percent are black. The percentage of white serial killers is nearly consistent with the share of the overall white population in the United States; while the black share is nearly double their overall population in the country.

So to those knowledgeable about serial killer demographics, such as those on the Atlanta Child Murders Task Force, Williams' arrest and conviction was not so strange.

In fact, the Atlanta Child Murders case was one of the first in the United States where the new art, or science, depending on how one views the discipline, was utilized extensively. Profilers on the Task Force, as well as other notable profilers not working on the case, argued that the killer was more than likely black, which of course turned out to be true.

Profilers also played a critical role in Wayne Williams' capture.

The profilers on the Task Force carefully tracked the killer's movement and accurately predicted where he would dump his victims. The Task Force then staked out the areas the profilers noted, which led to Williams' arrest on a bridge in the middle of the night.

Many in Atlanta, and eventually throughout the United States, found it difficult to believe that a young black man would kill so many black children and young men. These doubts inevitably led to conspiracy theories which were explored by a host of journalists, lawyers and eventually even Williams himself.

Early in the killings, long before Williams was even a suspect, many in the black community thought that the killer was white. Eventually, this idea gave way to conspiracy theories believing that Ku Klux Klan was responsible for the murders as part of a bizarre plot to start a race war.

When Williams finally went on trial, the public was able to see the mountain of circumstantial and physical evidence against him. This, in turn, dampened many of the conspiracy theories, leading most in the black community to believe the right man was behind bars

However, the conspiracy theories resurfaced during the mid-1980s when Williams filed appeals and again in the mid-2000s when a law enforcement official suggested that there may be some credibility to the claims. The conspiracy claims made for good news copy and even fiction, which kept the story going, but there was little substance to the claims.

There was no evidence of a Klan conspiracy has ever been uncovered and nearly all legitimate law enforcement officials believe there is nothing to the claim. There are still many unresolved issues concerning the Atlanta Child Murders.

Members of the Task Force publicly stated, even days before Williams was arrested, there was probably more than one killer involved. Still other Task Force members have stated in the years after the killings, although Williams was certainly guilty of the murders for which he was convicted, he was more than likely not guilty of all the killings.

These statements have led to claims that Williams may have had help with his killing spree. Although there is no evidence that Williams had a partner or partners, some believe that the slightly built, nerdy looking guy couldn't have killed so many people on his own.

The unanswered questions led to more questions and soon other conspiracy theories were forwarded to explain the extraordinarily high kill count. Similar to the Klan theory, many of these other theories were outlandish and not backed by any real hard evidence, yet were believed by a vocal minority of the population.

Even when debunked, conspiracy theories never go away totally.

Finally, there were questions about how many of the murders were possibly domestic related, but made to look like it was the work of the Atlanta Child Killer. Unfortunately, the world is full of demented people who will take advantage of any situation, no matter how bad it is, to satisfy a grim desire. Because of this sad truth, there is a good possibility that at least a couple of the murders attributed to Williams were actually committed in a domestic situation.

The lingering questions have ensured the Atlanta Child Murders case will not be forgotten any time soon. Wayne Williams has also done his part to keep the case in the public eye by giving interviews, which have been routinely dissected by experts ranging in such fields as law to body language.

Truly, the Atlanta Child Murders left a major scar on the city of Atlanta which will more than likely never totally heal.

CHAPTER 1:
The Killings Begin

In the summer of 1979, Atlanta, Georgia was a city with a long history that was in transition. It was once the symbol of the "Old South," having been burned to the ground in 1864 at the beginning of Union General William Tecumseh Sherman's notorious "March to the Sea" during the Civil War. In the decades after the war, Atlanta quickly rebounded by becoming an economic center as a railroad and transportation hub, but also as a symbol of resistance to the North and liberal ideas such as racial integration.

During the late 1950s, Atlanta became fertile recruiting ground for the newly formed National States' Rights Party, which advocated racial segregation as part of its platform. Led by firebrand J.B. Stoner, the NSRP established a strong presence in Atlanta, conducting several demonstrations and acts of sabotage.

In 1958, five men linked to the NSRP were indicted for but never convicted of bombing a Jewish synagogue in Atlanta.

Atlanta was also the home of Lester Madox, who built his political cache as an unapologetic segregationist on his way to the governorship of Georgia.

Despite its symbol as a place of resistance against the North, Atlanta was also the home of Martin Luther King Junior, which also made it an important center in the Civil Rights movement of the 1950s and 1960s. King and many other leaders from the Civil Rights era not only made Atlanta their homes, but also used the city as a base from which to launch their campaigns.

Once the smoke of the turbulent 1960s lifted, Atlanta's leaders placed the city in a prime position to grow economically. The international airport became one of the most used commercial ports in the United States, anchored by Delta Airlines, and Coca-Cola employed thousands. Atlanta suddenly transformed from a sleepy southern city to a cosmopolitan metropolis within a couple of decades.

The 1970s witnessed a large wave of "white flight" across the United States where white middle-class families migrated to the suburbs in the wake of desegregation and the Civil Rights movement. Cities with large black communities, such as Atlanta, were affected more than others, as they changed from having an almost even share of white and black residents to overwhelmingly black overnight.

Although statistically speaking Atlanta's black community was better off than many other large, urban black communities, crime and unemployment were commonplace.

The phenomenon of single mother households also started to become common among all ethnic groups in the United States during the 1970s, but even more so in the black community.

Along with the demographic changes came a major shift in political power. After whites began leaving the inner city *en masse*, the number of white elected officials precipitously dropped. The result was that by the mid-1970s, Atlanta had a black mayor, a predominantly black city council, and what was quickly becoming a mainly black police force.

This was the cultural and historical backdrop in which the Atlanta Child Murders took place.

Edward Smith and Alfred Evans

The first two attributed victims of the Atlanta Child Murders series had a number of commonalities concerning their age, appearance, and backgrounds, but there were also a couple of significant differences in the way they were killed.

On July 21, 1979, Edward Smith was a fourteen-year-old boy who loved watching and playing sports. He was quite athletic and well-built for his age and could've certainly given Wayne Williams more than he asked for in a fight, if not taken the older man altogether.

But Wayne Williams, like most successful serial killers, focused on his victims' weaknesses.

Edward Smith's weakness was poverty.

He was raised in the East Lake Meadows housing project in southwest Atlanta, barely knowing his father and having little supervision from his mother.

Smith would do any odd jobs and errands he could around the

neighborhood to earn a little cash, which sometimes put him around nefarious individuals, but the street-smart kid was always careful. According to his friends, he usually made good choices on the streets and didn't let people take advantage of him. A person usually had to earn his trust with Edward.

His friends and family said he would've never got into a car with someone he didn't trust.

On the night in question, Smith was feeling happy because he made a little money that day doing some odd jobs so,, he brought his girlfriend out on a date to the local roller-skating rink. The two left the rink around ten pm, said their goodbyes, and went their separate ways.

Edward Smith was never again seen alive.

Thirteen-year-old Alfred Evans was also an athletic kid who grew up on the tough streets of Atlanta with little adult supervision. Evans grew up not far from Smith and also did a number of odd jobs around his neighborhood to make some spending money. Sometimes Evans would stay out all night, so when he didn't come home on the night of July 25, 1979, his mother was not immediately worried.

Evans' mother called the police the next day, but the case was not prioritized since the boy had been known to run away in the past. Alfred was also known to run with a rough crowd who were known to experiment with drugs and were said to be involved in petty crimes.

The police told Alfred's mother that he would probably come home in a day or two and that she shouldn't worry.

Then on July 28, 1979, the bodies of Smith and Evans were discovered together in a wooded area in southwest Atlanta.

The police were not immediately sure what they had. The coroner's examination of the boys bodies revealed that Smith was shot and killed with a .22 caliber gun in the back, while Evans had been strangled. The investigators then learned that the boys had disappeared on separate nights and it wasn't clear if they even knew each other.

They reasoned that it was just a coincidence that their bodies were dumped in the same location. After all, it was a high-crime neighborhood and as tragic as it was, those sorts of things happen.

Still, the murder of two children in such a short span was rare, even in Atlanta, so they began combing the streets looking for leads. Not long after the bodies were discovered, Atlanta detectives received a tip that both murders were drug-related. The tipster said that both of the boys were hanging out at a house smoking marijuana a few days before they went missing.

Although friends and family members of both boys denied they were involved in drugs, the police thought the lead was credible.

The cases, though, were not followed up and were quickly forgotten.

Milton Harvey and Yusef Bell

The next black child to disappear off Atlanta's streets was fourteen-year-old Milton Harvey. Milton was last seen going to the bank for his mother on September 4, 1979, but never returned. His badly decomposed body was discovered in a wooden area in November 1979.

Although Milton Harvey's mother reported him missing, the police thought that it was just another routine runaway from a typically dysfunctional family. The report was filed but not followed up. At this point it was clear that a pattern was emerging, but it was not one that the Atlanta Police immediately noticed.

The killer didn't strike again until the evening of October 21, 1979. The victim that evening was a nine-year-old boy named Yusef Bell, who was playing in the street with some friends when an elderly neighbor asked him to run an errand.

Bell's neighbor asked him if he would make the two block walk to the neighborhood convenience store to buy some snuff for her. Like Smith and Evans, Bell would often do such errands for neighborhoods for a little extra cash and/or some goodies from the store. On this night, the neighbor promised to let Bell keep whatever change was left, which wouldn't have been much, but enough to buy some candy or a couple of sodas.

Witnesses reported seeing Bell in the store buying the snuff and some candy and he was even seen walking home from the store.

But then, just like with Edward Smith, Yusef Bell vanished on the streets of Atlanta.

Although the details of Yusef Bell's disappearance were very similar to the first two cases, one of the major differences was that Camille Bell, Yusef's mother, was not willing to let her son's disappearance be written off as a simple runaway case. Yusef was not a problem child, she argued, and he had never run away before.

Camille Bell knew that something awful had happened to her son on his way back from the store.

"And nobody saw anybody do anything, or anything, but they did see him come back across the street and that was the last we saw him," said Camille Bell.

Yusef Bell's decomposed body was discovered a month later in an abandoned school. The cause of death was determined to have been strangulation.

As Camille Bell continued to pressure the Atlanta authorities, the idea that there was a serial killer hunting Atlanta's black youth began to spread throughout the city. The idea was still a whisper in late 1979 and early 1980, but more and more people were talking about it. The media had still not picked up on the "Atlanta Child Murders Case" officially and local law enforcement did not yet make a statement about any of the abductions and murders being connected, but there was little doubt in many people's minds that they were.

And the killer was also apparently feeling the heat.

After murdering Bell, the killer went into a cooling off period of almost four months. As mentioned in Chapter 1, part of the definition of a serial killer is that the killer goes into at least one cooling off period, with the first one usually being early in the series. A major reason why the killer goes into a cooling off period early in the series doesn't have to do with a sudden twinge of morality on the killer's part—serial killers by definition have no sense of morality or empathy—but it has more to do with the fear of getting caught.

Most serial killers fantasize about murder for years, if not their entire lives, before committing their first murder, so when they actually make that monumental step they are faced with the reality of what they have done. Many serial killers lay low during this period and go about their normal lives while meticulously checking news reports, if there are any, about the investigation.

For Wayne Williams, late 1979 and early 1980 was a time when he focused on his music career and his attempts to form a boy band.

But for serial killers, cooling off periods are temporary. Sooner or later the urge to kill reasserts itself.

When spring came in 1980, Atlanta's child killer came out of hibernation by reducing the city to a state of terror that would last for over a year.

It is believed that the killer's first post-cooling off period victim was twelve-year-old Angel Lenair. The attribution of this murder to Wayne Williams and the Atlanta Child Murders is still somewhat controversial, because she was a girl and all but one other of the victims were male. In other ways her murder fit perfectly with the M.O. of all the other Atlanta Child Murders.

Lenair went to run some errands for her family on the night of March 4, 1980 but never returned. Her body was found six days later in a wooded area and was determined to have been strangled to death with a cord and possibly sexually assaulted.

The case certainly diverged from the others in some ways, but due to the similarities of the manner of death and disposal of the body, Angel Lenair was later placed on the list of Atlanta Child Murder victims.

One week after Angel Lenair was abducted, ten-year-old Jeffrey Mathis disappeared from his Atlanta neighborhood. Mathis was last seen walking to a local convenience store to buy cigarettes for his mother, but like most of the other initial victims, he was never again seen alive.

Jeffrey Mathis' badly decomposed body was discovered in a wooded area a year later.

At this point, the secret could no longer be contained that a serial killer was targeting black youths, mainly boys, on Atlanta's streets. The case slowly began to attract media attention and was eventually dubbed by the press as the "Atlanta Child Murders" case.

Although by the middle of 1980 the authorities believed that there were one or more serial killers operating in Atlanta, catching the killer, or killers, would be no easy task. This was several years before DNA profiling was available to law enforcement, few businesses had closed-circuit television cameras, and the victims all came from neighborhoods that were traditionally leery of cooperating with the police.

And the primary suspect turned out to be a wily and extremely cunning individual.

CHAPTER 2:
Wayne Bertram Williams

Serial killers become infamous for a number of reasons. Some, such as Henry Lee Lucas, become renowned for their extraordinarily high kill count, whether real or exaggerated, while others, such as Jeffrey Dahmer, are remembered for their extreme brutality and willingness to transgress every human taboo.

But the reality is, many serial killers are remembered for their personalities.

Ted Bundy is remembered as much for defending himself in court and the later interviews he gave to the press than for how many women he killed or how he killed them.

The same is true for notable female serial killer Aileen Wuornos, whose numerous bizarre interviews and statements kept fans of true crime wanting to see more.

Perhaps this stems from fictional portrayals of Hannibal Lecteresqe serial killers who outfox the authorities with their superior intellect and do so in high style. Besides the Hannibal Lecter character, most fictional accounts of serial killers portray them as highly intelligent, sophisticated, often physically attractive, and extremely charismatic. Although these traits are not applicable to most serial killers, when one such as Ted Bundy possesses them, the result is sometimes a media sensation.

Wayne Williams may not be Hannibal Lecter, but in many ways he is a serial killer who seems tailor-made for television. He occasionally gives interviews to the press proclaiming his innocence, which is always interesting due to a combination of his engaging personality and often bizarre theories he advocates concerning his background and who he really thinks murdered all the victims.

Williams is also articulate and has at least an average IQ, so he is able to present his lies and excuses in a believable and often interesting manner.

And although Williams may not seem particularly charismatic or charming, he comes across as approachable and not at all what one would think of as a cold-blooded killer.

An examination of his background reveals that Wayne Williams is an intriguing personality, but also one who fits the serial killer mold perfectly.

Early Life

Wayne Williams was born in 1958 in what was at that time, for the most part, still a racially segregated Atlanta. His was raised in the Dixie Hills neighborhood in southwest Atlanta, which was also where he was living when he was arrested for murder.

The Dixie Hills neighborhood also happened to be where many of the Atlanta Child Murders victims lived.

The neighborhood itself was quite unique and indicative of the segregation era. Many black-owned businesses served as anchors in Dixie Hills, with many of the middle and even upper-class proprietors living in the neighborhood. By the late 1960s, large government housing projects began to surround the neighborhood, leading to massive socio-economic changes.

As white flight took place in Atlanta during the 1970s, many upper- and middle-income black families actually followed their white neighbors to the suburbs. Dekalb County, which is located just east of Atlanta and Fulton County, became one of the major landing spots for many of these black families. Eventually, inner-city neighborhoods such as Dixie Hills became poorer and more crime ridden as a result.

Besides the income that left Dixie Hills and other similar neighborhoods during the 1970s, a major cultural shift also took place.

Most of the families that left the neighborhood were two parent units and they were replaced by primarily single mothers living in the housing projects.

Although the socio-economic transition in Wayne Williams' childhood neighborhood was severe and quick, some families, such as his, decided to stay put. The Williams family's home was paid off, so they decided to stay and make the best of it and they reasoned that things had not deteriorated so bad and that the neighborhood was still relatively safe.

For Wayne Williams, his childhood was pretty non-eventful compared to most other serial killers.

Both of Wayne's parents worked as school teachers and remained married until death. There is no evidence to suggest that the Williams parents were abusive in any way toward each other. All sources indicate that Homer and Faye Williams had a good relationship and kept an orderly, clean home. There was no illicit drug use in the Williams home and alcohol consumption was rare and done in moderation.

There is also no evidence that Wayne was abused by his parents, in fact, all sources suggest that if anything he was doted on by his parents. Since he was an only child, Wayne's parents bought him toys, and later electronic gadgets, that kids in his neighborhood could only dream of.

And because his parents were teachers, they encouraged him in all his academic pursuits, which for Wayne was primarily electronics and music.

In school, Wayne was at the top of his class. In later interviews after he was convicted of murder, Wayne Williams' teachers had nothing but good things to say about his academic career. He was a consistent "A" student who was described as quiet, intelligent, respectful, and helpful. According to tests he was given, Williams also had an above average IQ.

But there were still some things that were just a little "off."

Young Wayne Williams was a consummate loner, preferring to spend time by himself over other kids his age, male or female. And Williams' studious nature and glasses sometimes earned him a healthy dose of bullying from his peers, which is known to be brutal at times among black American youths.

But Williams used his intelligence and verbal skills to get out of most situations without violence. Wayne could engage in the black American pastime of verbal one-upmanship known as "the dozens" as well as any other kid at his school, which earned him respect and the right to be left alone.

The result was that although a loner, Williams was a somewhat popular kid. His quick whit was enough to keep most of the bullies off his back and when that didn't work he could help others with their electronic gadgets.

Wayne Williams learned at an early point in his life how to manipulate situations to fit his needs.

Williams attended Frederick Douglass High School where he graduated at the top of his class as student council president. His grades and test scores were good enough to get him into most of the major regional universities, with many scholarship offers, but he instead decided to stay home and become an entrepreneur.

Wayne would later take some classes at Georgia State University, which is located in Atlanta, after he graduated, studying business and finance, but his heart just wasn't in the regimented discipline of college life.

In 1976, Wayne Williams was a young man with big dreams who seemingly had the world in his grasp.

Unfortunately, less than three years later he would put dozens of Atlanta's children in his grasp and leave their dead bodies scattered in vacant lots and rivers around the city.

The Talent Agent

While Williams was in grade school, he developed a deep interest in electronics and music. As mentioned earlier, he displayed an exceptional aptitude for the mechanics of electronic equipment and he developed an appreciation for music. Williams especially enjoyed rhythm and blues, Motown, and any type of Soul music. Like many people of the time, his favorite band was the Jackson Five, whom Wayne hoped to emulate in some way.

Despite Wayne Williams' love of music, it became obvious that he had no natural talent to be a musician.

Still, Wayne Williams was a determined kid so he wouldn't let that hinder a potential music career.

While Williams may not have had an ear for music, he certainly had an aptitude for electronics. Before Williams was a teenager, he often took radios apart and put them back together, which then evolved into him helping fix friends' and family members' radios and other small electronic devices.

Wayne Williams also discovered his latent business talents at this time.

When he wasn't fixing his friends' family's radios for free, he made some extra cash by charging for his services. By the time he was in high school, Williams could demand nice fees for his mechanical services.

As noted above, Williams parents encouraged his interests, so when they saw that he possessed a fair amount of mechanical acumen and had an interest in music and broadcasting, they gave him the money to start his own radio station in their home. Such an investment would often be a waste, considering that the interests of sixteen-year-old kids are capricious to say the least.

But Wayne Williams was different in this respect.

During his late teens, Wayne worked at area radio stations part-time to learn both the technical and financial aspects of the radio business, often impressing the adults he met.

"He was a bit old for his age," said one Atlanta radio person, noting not only how articulate Wayne Williams was, but also mature. Williams had clear career goals that he was pursuing while most boys his age were more interested in girls and/or hanging out with their buddies.

It was precisely Wayne Williams' articulate, smooth-talking persona that helped him kill so many people and get away with it for so long. It is also that persona that still convinces people that he is actually innocent.

By 1976, Williams decided to combine his knowledge of electronics and the music business with his personality to make money as a talent agent.

As Williams made more and more contacts in Atlanta's radio and music scenes, he meticulously wrote each one of them down on his resume, although it would later be determined that many of the people claimed to have never met him. Still, as Williams compiled his extensive list of industry contacts, real and imaginary, he was able to convince several young people that he was a legitimate "talent agent."

Williams' interest was primarily in young boys, which he later claimed was because he was attempting to replicate the success of the Jackson Five.

His appeal to the kids would usually be that he was putting a band together and that he would put up the money for an initial demo that would be sent to various music producers who he knew. Once the band was signed to a label, then they would be paid.

After Williams gathered together some talent that he thought could be hitmakers, he would have the kids audition in either his home studio or one of the many music studios in the Atlanta area.

Although Williams was well remembered by Atlanta area music producers, most were not impressed.

"To my best recollection he auditioned young kids for a group that never existed," said Kathy Andrews, the co-owner of Atlanta Studios where Williams cut demo tapes.

His poor ear for music eventually resulted in bankrupting his parents, but Williams saw the situation differently.

During an interview in prison, Williams said that although none of his acts made it big, he was on the verge of doing so.

"So I actually started off working with some of the bigger local bands that we had. As a matter of fact, when Alisha Bridges did her thing, 'I Love the Nightlight,' I happened to be in the studio when she did it," said Williams later from prison.

Williams attempts to make it big in the music business at first glance appears to be a failed, yet innocent, attempt to establish a career; but a closer look at one particular band he formed seems to have foreshadowed his true calling.

Gemini

Wayne Williams' 1970s brainchild was a Jackson Fiveesque band that he called Gemini. The name of the group seemed perfectly in line with the astrology craze of the period, but it also betrayed a bit of Williams' ego – he was born on May 27 under the Gemini astrological sign.

Williams spread the word of his band project by word of mouth and also printed up hundreds of flyers that he distributed in arcades, skating rinks, shopping malls, and just about anywhere where young black boys hung out.

Many of the places also happened to be where kids were abducted during the Atlanta Child Murders case.

According to Williams, Gemini was supposed to be a top-shelf, professional group and the flyers were supposed to reflect that.

"When the flyer came about, when we made the decision with Gemini not be, I guess you could say a chitlin circuit band," said Williams from prison.

Williams also later claimed that his work with Gemini gave him access to most of the public schools in Atlanta and that the teachers and administrators were only too eager to work with him.

"The first thing we did was, I contacted on our letterhead every single public school music program in the city of Atlanta. We wrote them and we actually visited all the music teachers and when I say we I mean myself and also my assistant Carla Bailey," recalled Williams. "And we had release forms if they were under eighteen a parent had to come to the audition or sign a release form."

Like many of Williams' claims, his contact with Atlanta public school officials cannot be verified, nor can his claim that he contacted the Atlanta Child Murder Task Force in 1980 shortly after he started auditions for Gemini. Although it is unlikely that Williams contacted the Task Force, because he is such a narcissist he may in fact have done so. It is in the nature of serial killers to play "cat and mouse" games with the police and as will be shown later, Williams also liked to take part in these sort of games.

He may have also contacted the Task Force to insert himself into the investigation.

Besides playing cat and mouse games with the police, it is also not uncommon for serial killers and other high-profile criminals to insert themselves into police investigations. One of the more notable examples of this is the "Co-ed Killer," Edmund Kemper, who killed ten people during the 1960s and 1970s in California. As the police were hot the trail of the Co-ed Killer, Kemper often gave his advice and theories to officers working the case.

It would follow Williams' personality that he would also attempt to insert himself into the investigation.

It is interesting and important to note that although Williams attempted to form a band comprised mainly of minor aged boys, he was nocturnal by nature, doing most of his business, legal and illegal, at night.

The Night Owl

Millions of people are by nature night people. They prefer to work at night for a variety of reasons that are for the most part innocent, so being a night owl is not in itself proof of anything bad, but if you are accused of the Atlanta Child Murders it becomes another piece of circumstantial evidence against you.

Wayne Williams was a creature of the night.

"Being an ex-news reporter and all, you know, nighttime is me, that's the time I'm out most of the time," said Williams.

In that quote, Williams was referring to his job as a freelance accident scene photographer. Williams' love of electronics extended to photography, which was also a family business as Wayne's father also worked as a freelance photographer.

According to Williams, he would drive around Atlanta in his car all night, listening to his scanner and police band radio, until he would hear a call about a fire, murder, or another type of accident. He would then rush to the scene, take some photos, and go home and develop the film. Williams would then pick what he believed were the best pictures and sell them to the local newspapers.

Williams also had a video camera, long before most people even knew what a VCR was. He would do the same thing with the videos, but sell the disaster footage to the local television stations.

The work gave Williams a chance to learn about all the hangout spots in Atlanta, as well as any number of alleys and side streets one would have to know to evade prying eyes. This knowledge proved to be useful later to Williams as he prowled like a panther during the night, often, but not always evading the watchful eyes of witnesses.

Most importantly, the job allowed Williams to learn where all the vacant lots and wooded areas were—the kind that was perfect for dumping bodies—within the city limits. Williams also found out where some of the more isolated bridges were in the Atlanta metro area.

The types of bridges where bodies could be thrown off of in the middle of the night.

Truly, Wayne Williams learned how to use the nighttime to his advantage when he hunted his victims.

It is unknown if Williams did "dry runs" while he was on disaster calls. The authorities know, and Williams even admitted, that he handed out numerous flyers at night at many of the spots where children were abducted, which seems to at least suggest that he was "feeling out" certain locations. Due to Wayne Williams' intelligence and more organized nature, it would not be a stretch of the imagination to think that he probably took notes, at least mentally, when he visited these locations before he began killing.

It is also rumored, but not confirmed, that Williams cruised for men while he was working as a disaster scene photographer. No men have ever come forward to confirm they had a sexual relationship with Williams and only one woman has admitted having been involved with him.

Although Wayne Williams' sexuality still seems ambiguous, or perhaps he is even asexual, it played a role in his trial.

But what was perhaps the most perplexing aspect of his life, and in many ways the most damning, was the bizarre fantasy world he created.

The Fantasy World of Wayne Williams

Beneath the well-crafted façade that Wayne Williams presented to the public as an intelligent, ambitious young man, lurked a confused person who would say anything to impress people. As mentioned earlier, Williams often exaggerated, or outright lied, about his professional contacts and he also lied about other facts on his resume.

Although Wayne Williams was certainly a good student in high school, he claimed to be a member of several organizations, which he wasn't, including the National Honor Society and the Junior ROTC.

But perhaps most telling was his fixation to be an authority figure.

Williams was known to dress as a police officer and was even arrested in 1976, not long after he graduated from high school, for impersonating a police officer. Although the charge was dropped, Williams never gave up his replica police uniforms or the police light he kept in his car.

During the height of the Atlanta Child Murders case, a popular theory circulated that the killer, or killers, was either a member of law enforcement, or disguising himself as law enforcement, in order to get the children to go with him without a struggle. It would also explain how the killer was able to move about without being seen.

And Williams was said to play the role of a police officer quite well.

"He had acquired, for instance an uncanny ability to impersonate a police officer," said author Bernard Headley.

Williams also made other outlandish claims to people who often knew better.

For example, he once told acquaintance and successful black Atlanta businessman, Eustis Bailey, that he was once an Air Force fighter pilot. Wayne Williams was only twenty-two when he made the claim and overweight and nearsighted.

Wayne Williams was hardly "Top Gun" material.

Perhaps the most bizarre claim Williams has made was that he was trained as an operative for the Central Intelligence Agency (CIA).

During the 1970s, Williams told some of his associates from time to time that he was involved in covert training with the CIA, but that it was top secret and he couldn't give many details. He did tell anyone who listened that he was trained to kill with his hands, particularly choking and strangling people to death.

Most of these bizarre claims were forgotten until the 1990s when prison authorities confiscated a rambling manifesto from Williams' cell titled "Finding Myself."

Prison is in fact a place where many people become introspective and find god, or any other assorted metaphysical philosophies. Many people also find themselves in exercise or even a new, legitimate trade when they are incarcerated.

But Wayne Williams' screed had little to do with self-improvement and read more like a poor imitation of a Tom Clancy novel. In the writings, Williams claimed that he was recruited by a secretive black operation cell of the CIA when he was in high school, because of his good grades and demonstrated technical abilities.

According to Williams, the CIA made an offer that was too good to refuse.

He said that the CIA offered to train him, along with several other young black men, in the forests of northern Georgia for a program that would ultimately send him and the other trainees to hotspots in Africa. He would then either be offered full-time employment in the CIA or would be able to use his experience to work in the military or the private sector.

Williams said he agreed to enter the program and spent most of the summer after graduating from high school at a camp. He claimed that the CIA trained him in weapons, explosives, and hand to hand combat. The hand to hand combat primarily involved ways in which to kill a person through choke holds, the type of choke holds that were responsible for the deaths of many of the children in the Atlanta Child Murders case.

In a 2010 interview on CNN, journalist Soledad O'Brien challenged Williams about the writings, particularly the sections about hand to hand combat. Williams only responded to O'Brien by saying "you could kill someone with your hands" and then shut down the interview.

O'Brien was visibly disturbed by his response.

It's clear that Wayne Williams lives in a fantasy world and has delusions of grandeur, much like many other notorious serial killers. If Wayne Williams can look someone in the eye and not blink while telling such an enormous lie as him being a CIA operative, then it should be clear that he would lie about anything.

Perhaps what is more telling is that Williams was able to get a fair amount of people to believe his stories. By using his charm and intelligence, he was able to get people to follow along with his schemes and ideas, which was even easier to do with children, who often saw Wayne Williams as a way out of the ghetto.

CHAPTER 3:
More Murders

As the spring of 1980 progressed and the city neared the one-year anniversary of the beginning of the Atlanta Child Murders, investigators began to believe that they had a serious problem on their hands. The investigators began to look at each of the missing and murdered children as a whole and a number of patterns and similarities emerged.

Most of the missing and murdered children were pre-teen boys and all of them were black.

The murdered boys were nearly all strangled and dumped in either wooded or vacant lots, or abandoned building.

It was also believed that the crimes were sexual in nature, although no semen was found on the bodies and few showed any signs of trauma around the genitals.

With that said, it certainly looked like there was a pattern emerging, but there were still questions that investigators had concerning dissimilarities the murders.

The first attributed victim, Edward Smith, was shot instead of strangled. He was included with the other victims on the list because his body was found in the same location as Alfred Evans' corpse.

The difference in M.O. from the first and the majority of the rest of the murders should not come as that big of a surprise, though. Many serial killers "experiment" with their M.O. until they find one that works best. In the case of Edward Smith, it may simply have been that since he was Wayne Williams' first kill, Williams had to make sure that the job would get done. After all, Williams was not a very big guy, while Smith was quite fit and athletic.

And as will be discussed later, it appears that more than one of Williams' victims put up a fight.

Perhaps out of all the early murders attributed to Wayne Williams, the one that fits the least is the murder of Angel Lenair.

Lenair's abduction and murder was obviously anomalous because she was only one of two girls attributed to the Atlanta Child Murders – the other girl's case is even more doubtful and will be considered later – but also the manner in which she was murdered.

Although Angel Lenair was choked to death, it was determined that an electrical cord was the weapon. Most of the other victims are believed to have been manually strangled.

Lenair was also visibly sexually abused and a pair of panties that were not her own were shoved into her mouth.

For these reasons, many people doubt that Williams killed Lenair;

but it may just have been a case where he was getting sloppy.

Many serial killers get sloppy when they believe they won't get caught.

Getting Sloppy

Whether Williams killed Angel Lenair or not, the reality is that by the middle of 1980 the Atlanta Child Killer, who this author along with most in law enforcement believes is when Wayne Williams, began to get sloppy.

Every serial killer lacks empathy with his or her victims, and with greater society in general, and most are imbued with an incredible amount of arrogance.

Wayne Williams certainly fits that description.

When serial killers get away with a few murders they often have a tendency to get sloppy in their work. They believe that they are smarter and one step ahead of law enforcement. It is at this point when serial killers begin to get bolder with some of their killings, taunting the police and sometimes playing to the media.

It is also the point where they are most prone to make mistakes.

On May 18, 1980, Wayne Williams made what appeared to have been his first major mistakes.

On the evening in question, fourteen-year-old Eric Middlebrooks received a phone call at his mother's home. After talking on a phone for a few minutes, he left in a hurry on his bike and never returned.

Middlebrooks' body was discovered the next day in an alley behind a bar.

At first glance, Middlebrooks' murder didn't seem to fit with the others on the growing list: he had been bludgeoned to death and his body wasn't dumped in a wooded or vacant lot.

But other elements of his murder did fit with the Atlanta Child Murders.

Middlebrooks was a black male under the age of eighteen who was known to spend a lot of time on the streets of Atlanta. Like many of the other victims, Middlebrooks earned spending cash by doing odd jobs around the neighborhood, such as fixing bikes, which put him into contact with numerous people. Some of the people he came into contact with through his odd jobs were known to have criminal records and were overall shady characters.

But Eric was also a street-smart kid who knew Atlanta quite well. In fact, he was arguably more street smart and bigger than most of the early victims of the Atlanta Child Killer.

In other words, Eric Middlebrooks is the type of kid who could handle himself and for him to be murdered in the way he was suggested that there were either multiple attackers, he was ambushed, or the killer had won his confidence somehow.

The crime scene was quickly cordoned off and the forensic detectives began to do their work. Although technologies common today such as DNA profiling were not available in 1980, forensic detectives were still able to check fingerprints, when available, as well as other less exact biological evidence.

Blood evidence could be checked for types and hairs could be roughly matched.

These types of forensic sciences could help eliminate certain subjects and provide more evidence against others who matched, but they could not point to someone with certainty the way DNA profiling can today.

And there was a new forensic science that was becoming more accepted in law enforcement during the late 1970s and early 1980s – fiber analysis.

Fiber analysis is simply the examination of fibers left at a crime scene and their comparison with a potential source carpet or rug. Of course, in order for fiber analysis to work a suspect is needed, but the collection of any and all evidence at a crime scene is imperative in order to later match a suspect to the scene.

One particularly astute Atlanta PD crime scene detective named Bob Buffington knew about fiber analysis. When he examined Eric Middlebrooks' body at the crime scene he noticed a peculiar red fiber on the bottom of the boy's shoe.

At the time, Buffington didn't know if the fiber was important, but not wanting to miss a potential chance he bagged the fiber and filed it into evidence.

His colleagues were not immediately impressed with the evidence and actually teased him quite a bit about filing it.

"The lieutenant made a big joke out of it and told the rest of the squad that if I went over to the lieutenant's house and cleaned out the lint trap in his dryer we could probably clear out all the cases in the city of Atlanta," Buffington later recalled.

Still, the single fiber was sent to the Georgia Bureau of Investigation's (GBI) state crime lab where Larry Peterson analyzed it.

He was intrigued, but unable to do much with it at the time because he had no suspect and/or other carpets for which to match it. Still, Peterson thanked Buffington for his diligence and assured him that it was a good find. He knew that the discovery could break the Atlanta Child Murders case.

How Were there So Many?

One of the aspects of the Atlanta Child Murders case that baffled so many at the time, including law enforcement officers, was how the murderer was able to take so many children with few to no witnesses and for the most part without struggles. As bizarre theories swirled that Ku Klux Klan death squads were invading Atlanta's inner city in order to kidnap and murder random black children. Law enforcement officers, criminologists, and various other academics knew that something else was taking place.

The killer was a wolf in sheep's clothing.

The killer, or killers – as will be discussed later, law enforcement publicly acknowledged that there was a high probability of more than one killer up until Wayne Williams' arrest – was obviously someone who could walk in the victims' neighborhoods without arising suspicion. He was also someone who could easily ingratiate himself to the victims and get them to let their guards down.

The killer was also someone quite familiar with the bleak economic and cultural conditions of the inner city. He knew that there was a large number of young black boys who were willing to do odd jobs for cash with few questions asked. The killer also knew that many of these boys ran the streets at all hours for the most part unsupervised.

Wayne Williams fit the description on all counts.

It was in light of these facts, renowned serial killer expert Dr. Helen Morrison, who also happened to be one of the first such people to hold that title, suggested that the Atlanta Child Killer was black. By the time Morrison offered her input on the Atlanta Child Murders in 1980, she was known for her testimony on Illinois serial killer John Wayne Gacy's behalf. Morrison testified that although Gacy had committed the series of murders for which he was accused, he was insane and therefore not legally responsible.

The jury didn't agree with Morrison's assessment.

Despite the jury in Gacy's trial not agreeing with Morrison, her opinions about serial killers were still respected by academics, criminologists, and law enforcement members. After offering her opinion about the Atlanta Child Murders case unsolicited, the Task Force that was later formed questioned her officially about the patterns in which the killer dumped some of the bodies in rivers.

Once the Atlanta area authorities publicly announced that the first of several child abductions and murders were probably related, they also were quite open about their theories concerning how the killer was able to abduct so many victims.

"With my theory the person is not abducted, not kidnapped, not snatched off the street at that particular time, but is really going with somebody for something, at least at the instance they get into the car, they going to make some money, or they going to meet somebody, they're going, starting off willingly," said Lewis Slaton from the Fulton County DA's office.

Witnesses would later state that in a number of the abduction/murders the victims willingly got into the probable killer's car. The man driving was referred to as "Wayne" on more than one occasion.

It is now clear that when Wayne Williams was doing his nighttime freelance photography and dropping flyers off for Gemini at arcades and other kids' hangouts, he was really trolling for victims.

And in the spring of 1980 Wayne Williams was just getting started.

CHAPTER 4:
Heightened Alert

During the spring of 1980, the Atlanta Child Murders case made a drastic turn. It was at that time when the local Atlanta media first began reporting on the murders as connected and part of a series. Local investigative journalists did a good job probing and questioning local law enforcement about the case, which led to the story being picked up by the national and eventually the international press.

It was one of the first serial killer cases to be extensively covered in the modern era and was perhaps the first to be broadly reported on in real-time.

For many, it was truly the case of the century.

Still, there were many who doubted that a serial killer was preying on the black children of Atlanta, arguing that the city normally has a high crime rate, most of which was in the black community. Many people who held those sentiments lived in the suburbs of Cobb County and didn't have much of a positive view of inner-city Atlanta to begin with, but even many inhabitants in the inner city were confused about the situation.

Some thought there was a serial killer, who happened to be black, targeting black children, while others believed it was part of some larger racist conspiracy. There were others who agreed with their suburban counterparts that the killings were just part of the larger breakdown of society and the rising crime rate.

It seemed like everyone had an opinion, but few had credible answers.

But Bob Buffington knew that there were far too many children killed in the time span for it to be normal.

"There had been a sharp increase in the number of children under the age of fourteen who had been killed," said Buffington.

Buffington claims to have repeatedly brought the idea that the murders were connected to his boss at an early point, but he was repeatedly rebuffed. It's ridiculous to talk about a serial killer who targeted the city's black children he was told, and such theories could do more harm than good.

"And I truly think that there would be a panic," said Buffington recalling how his boss threatened to transfer him.

As Atlanta's law enforcement community quarreled about if there even was a crisis, never mind how to deal with it, the rate of the murders increased.

Expanding His Territory

Although some serial killers are itinerant and travel over great distances killing people, most prefer to hunt in a territory in which they are well acquainted. Only after mastering their techniques do they then expand their killings zones.

In the Atlanta Child Murders case, by June 1980 the murders started to become more frequent and over a larger area of the Atlanta metropolitan area.

Three child murders took place that month, of which two have been attributed to Williams.

Twelve-year-old Chris Richardson disappeared on the night of June 9, 1980 and was found later, strangled to death. Due to the victim's age, the manner in which he was murdered, and the fact that his body was discovered in a remote location, the murder was later attributed to Wayne Williams.

A seven-year-old girl named Latonya Wilson was the next child added to the list when she was abducted from her home on June 23. Although there are legitimate doubts as to whether Williams was connected to this case, which will be considered later, her skeletal remains were discovered in a vacant lot over a month later.

The day after Latonya Wilson disappeared, ten-year-old Aaron Wyche vanished from his Atlanta neighborhood. His body was found the next day beneath a train trestle in neighboring Dekalb County, Georgia. It was initially believed that Wyche was playing on the trestle and fell to his death, but a more complete autopsy revealed that he was probably strangled to death.

Wyche's family also told investigators that he had no reason being in the area where he was found as it was far from his home and he didn't have a bicycle. The investigators later theorized that Williams enticed Aaron Wyche to take a ride in his car and then killed him, before dumping his body in a remote location as he did with so many of Atlanta's other children.

At this point in the case, the fear that many of Atlanta's residents had slowly turned to frustration and even anger. There was talk of vigilante groups forming and people became more paranoid and less trusting of their neighbors. Many Atlantans, especially black inner city Atlantans, didn't know who to trust.

If the serial killer was black as they were being told, then he could be anyone—someone's father, brother, cousin, or friend. And if the killer was posing as law enforcement, or actually was in law enforcement, then things were even more complicated and frustrating.

At this point in the case, many Atlantans, even adults, rarely left their homes.

The adults weren't necessarily scared of being the Atlanta Child Killer's next victim, but more so of being accused of being the killer.

The frustration, fear, and tension in the city of Atlanta could be cut with a knife.

STOP

When Yusef Bell was murdered, his mother Camille went through the typical grieving process, but she also decided to do something to bring the plight of Atlanta's children to the public's attention. Joined by other victims' mothers, such as Willie Mae Mathis and Venus Taylor, the women formed an organization they called the Committee to Stop Children's Murders or STOP.

From the start, STOP focused its energies on two fronts: first they made sure to tell their story to the press by giving press conferences and media interviews whenever a new body was discovered. Although the organization eventually added professional staff, the members usually handled the press themselves

Second, STOP pressured local enforcement to keep working on the cases. They did this through a combination of increased and persistent media pressure, but also by making regular contact with law enforcement officers who were working the case.

Although not all of the members of STOP had the same theories about the Atlanta Child Murders, with some even believing that Wayne Williams was innocent, they were all united in their effort to bring an end to the murders of Atlanta's black youth.

The mothers of STOP gave numerous interviews to the press, urging the police to step up their efforts, which finally paid off in the summer of 1980

The Task Force Is Created

As the body count climbed in the spring of 1980 and it became apparent to most in Atlanta that a serial killer was hunting the city's black youth, an unofficial task force formed. The Atlanta Police Department began coordinating their efforts with the Fulton County Sheriff's Department, the Dekalb County Sheriff's Department, and the GBI in order to catch the killer.

The increased media attention in the summer, along with the efforts of STOP, finally led to city officials officially announcing the formation of a task force.

On July 17, 1980, Atlanta Mayor Maynard Jackson announced the formation of the Special Police Task Force on Missing and Murdered Children at a press conference. The mayor told the press that by making the task force official, they would not only be able to better pool their resources but would also increase the amount of resources in the case.

In terms of manpower, the number of officers involved rose to 103, which included several FBI agents.

Besides the official Task Force, there were also scores of other individuals who dedicated their time and resources to helping capture the Atlanta Child Murderer. Some of these people were ordinary citizens, which will be discussed later, but others were seasoned law enforcement professionals such as Chet Dettlinger.

In 1980, Dettlinger was an ex-police officer who once served as a public safety commissioner and a consultant to the Justice

Department. Dettlinger assembled a team of other former law enforcement officers to offer their expertise on the Atlanta Child Murders case apart from the Task Force.

Dettlinger and his team eventually came up with a "List" of victims, which deviated somewhat from the official list—some victims on the official list were not included in Dettlinger's and others on Dettlinger's list were not among the official twenty-eight victims.

Along with the list, Dettlinger created a geographic profile of the victims that mapped out where all the victims were taken from and where their bodies were found. Dettlinger even claimed to be able to predict where the next victims would come from and when he proved to be accurate, some suspicion fell on him.

After being questioned by the Task Force, Dettlinger was cleared of any involvement in the murders. Once the FBI realized that Dettlinger offered valuable insight into the case, the Task Force invited Dettlinger to join in an official capacity.

But no matter how accurate Dettlinger's predictions were, they weren't able to stop the killings.

Mayor Jackson tried to reassure the city that they were doing everything in their power to catch the killer, or killers, and that it was only a matter of time before he was caught. With that said, there was a certain amount of desperation coming from Jackson. He seemed unsure of himself and let slip on more than one occasion just how far they were from identifying the killer

"Someone out there knows what we're looking for, knows who's doing this insane series of acts," said Jackson.

The Task Force was augmented by a number of agents from the FBI, such as renowned profiler Ray Hazelwood, who was brought to Atlanta to put some fresh eyes on the case. By 1980, Hazelwood had already worked on a number of kidnapping and serial murder cases so his experience was vital.

Since Hazelwood was a profiler, he needed to travel around the city of Atlanta in order to get a "sense" of what was taking place. Unlike how profilers are often portrayed in movies and on television using borderline psychic abilities, true police and FBI profilers employ a logical course by which they develop a suspect profile. Like Dettlinger did with his geographic profile, Hazelwood and the other full-time profilers on the task force employed a variety of methods to determine the killer's next move.

Profilers often begin with the victims, connecting similarities and ruling out differences not only in their backgrounds, but also the manner in which they were murdered.

Other factors are also considered such as the neighborhoods where the murders took place and the places where the bodies were discovered.

In other words, profilers look for patterns that the killer has been using. Once a pattern has been discerned, not only can the profilers make an educated guess about where and when the killer will strike next, but also other aspects about the killer's background including his race, age, socio-economic background etc.

After examining the case from his office in Washington, Hazelwood made the trip to Atlanta in late 1980 to see some of the neighborhoods for himself.

Hazelwood was met by two black Atlanta Police Department detectives, who offered to drive him around neighborhoods where some of the victims lived. Almost immediately, Hazelwood's profile began to take shape.

"As soon as we turned onto that street everything stopped. . . I said what's going on . . . they said laughingly that's because we have a honkey in a car," said Hazelwood in a later interview about the case.

The FBI profiler immediately informed the Task Force that the killer, or killers, was almost certainly black. There was virtually no way that a white serial killer, never mind a crew of Klansmen, could repeatedly enter some of these neighborhoods without being noticed.

Other members of the Task Force agreed with the assessment.

John Glover, who was the FBI chief in Atlanta at the time, and black, publicly agreed with Hazelwood's profile and stated.

"The killer is someone who is invisible in the black community."

The fact that the Atlanta Child Killer was black certainly went a long way in answering how the killer was able to so easily kill so many, seemingly without much struggle. Still, it didn't completely answer the question. The overwhelming majority of crime in the black community is black on black, so although the killer being black may have meant he was able to move unseen, it didn't explain how many of the murdered children, who were street smart and intimately familiar with crime, would have willingly gone with a stranger.

As already discussed, Wayne Williams was able to use a combination of his quick wits and connections in the music business to lure some of the children into his car, but that probably wasn't the situation in every case.

Former Fulton County, Georgia prosecutor Jack Mallard told the media that he and the Task Force believed that the killer was also using another ruse to abduct his victims.

"Some of us thought that perhaps it could be a police officer or someone perceived to be a police officer," said Mallard.

Wayne Williams just so happened to have replica police uniforms and a police light in his car.

The case continued to garner significant national media attention, leading to an announcement on November 5, 1980 by United States Attorney General Benjamin Civiletti. During a press conference on that day, Civilietti announced that the FBI was cooperating with local, county, and state law enforcement agencies and that case was now being followed by President Ronald Reagan.

The federal government was now on the hunt for the Atlanta Child killer.

CHAPTER 5:
No End in Sight

The formation of the Task Force was welcomed news to most in Atlanta. People were generally optimistic that with 103 law enforcement officers working on the case, including many seasoned FBI agents, that it wouldn't be long before the Atlanta Child murderer was captured.

Instead, the killings picked up in pace.

It was almost as if Williams viewed the Task Force's formation as a challenge: it would be up to him to prove that he could keep killing with impunity. This was a trait that Williams shared with most notable serial killers—an extreme hubris whereby he thought that not only were his victims far beneath him, but also the police.

Wayne Williams was going to prove that the Task Force couldn't stop his killing spree.

The next victim to be abducted and murdered during the summer of 1980 was nine-year-old Anthony Carter. The evening of July 5, 1980 was a hot one in the city, which often meant that kids were prone to be outside instead of in hot, stuffy houses and apartments with no air-conditioning. Despite knowing about the dangers of the Atlanta Child Killer, there were plenty of kids out that night in Anthony Carter's neighborhood having water fights, playing hide and seek, and generally oblivious to the dangers all around them.

Anthony Carter's mother was hesitant to let him play outside that night, but he reassured her that he would be with a group of kids from the neighborhood.

Anthony and his friends played hide and seek that night and stayed out well past curfew, for those who actually did have curfews. During the middle of one of their early morning games, Anthony Carter disappeared into thin air.

His mother and others in the neighborhood worried that he had become the next victim of the Atlanta Child Killer, so a call was made to the police. Anthony Carter was found stabbed to death in a vacant warehouse the next day.

Just over three weeks later, the killer struck again.

The victim this time was eleven-year-old Earl Terrel. Like many of the other boys who were abducted and murdered before him, Terrel was a street-smart kid who had little adult supervision. He ran the streets at all hours of the night, but was big for his age and could handle himself if need be.

Despite his age, Earl Terrel was not normally the victim type.

Earl was not only street smart, but he was also known to be a bit of a troublemaker. Although he had not been involved in anything major before July 1980, he was known to be a discipline problem in school and somewhat of a tough guy around kids his own age.

But the Atlanta Child Murders was not a normal case and all it took for a kid to become a victim is one wrong move into the waiting arms of Wayne Williams.

On the afternoon of July 30, 1980, Terrel and some of his friends went to the local public pool to swim and meet some of their other friends. Not long after arriving at the pool, Terrel was kicked out for causing problems with some other kids and threatening a lifeguard.

Earl told his friends that he was going to walk home, but he instead became the next victim on the growing list.

Terrel's aunt later claimed that she received a phone call from a man claiming he had Earl. The tip was followed up but nothing came of it. Earl's body was later found in a wooded area, having been strangled to death.

Saturday Searches

By the fall of 1980, the people of Atlanta were on edge and some were ready to take the law into their own hands. The Task Force didn't seem to be any closer to catching the killer, even with a hefty reward offered, which led to the conspiracy theories running rampant. Not only did the Klan theory resurface about that time, but there was also talk about a high-level government coverup. It was never explained exactly what the government was covering up and why they were interested in the murders in the first place, but it didn't stop people from talking.

Some people also talked about forming vigilante groups.

One group that actually did form was known as the "Bat Patrol." The Bat Patrol originated in the public housing projects known as Techwood Homes, which as located just to the west of downtown Atlanta near the campus of Georgia Tech University. The high-crime apartment complexes were leveled in the mid-1990s to make room for the 1996 Olympics, but before they were they acquired quite a reputation in the city of Atlanta.

The Bat Patrol was so named because residents of Techwood Homes traveled together in groups, armed with bats, in order to keep the Atlanta Child Killer at bay.

It didn't work.

Not long after the Bat Patrol was formed, the first adult victim in the Atlanta Child Murders case, twenty-one-year-old Eddie Duncan, disappeared on March 20, 1981 and his body was discovered on April 8, 1981 in the Chattahoochee River.

Others used the case to get their names in the headlines.

Political leaders and "community activists" came out of the woodwork in late 1980 to give their opinion on who was committing the murders and what should be done to stop them. Most of these people had few constructive things to offer and only brought back up conspiracy theories that had been, for the most part, disproved by law enforcement.

There was, though, a renewed spirit of civic duty in some neighborhoods.

Besides the Bat Patrol at Techwood Homes, legitimate neighborhood watch associations became more common and in many neighborhoods it was rare to see children out after dark, and never alone.

The city of Atlanta announced a citywide curfew in the fall of 1980 just before Halloween. Although the curfew didn't end the murder of children in the city, no kids were killed during Halloween.

A number of suburbs surrounding Atlanta that were unaffected by the Atlanta Child Murders also enacted curfews for minors in an effort to keep the murderous scourge from entering their cities.

Finally, the Atlanta city council decided to do its part when it organized "Saturday Searches" in October 1980. The Saturday Searches involved volunteers getting together to search wooded areas, vacant lots, and deserted buildings for victims of the Atlanta Child murderer around Atlanta every Saturday.

Many had their doubts, but the first weekend turned up the body of Latonya Wilson. Three more bodies were found during the Saturday Searches in 1980. Although the program turned out to be a success, it was most unfortunate.

Volunteers would have plenty of more bodies to find beginning in 1981.

Wayne Williams was about to up his game.

One Victim a Week

When the world celebrated the New Year in 1981, the city of Atlanta's celebrations were notably subdued. Usually the city would spend a considerable amount of money on New Year's festivities, attracting tens of thousands of people to the downtown area. In 1981, though, the crowds were noticeably smaller and there was far less happening.

The Atlanta Child Killer was beginning to affect Atlanta's economy.

Just two days later, on January 3, Wayne Williams decided to celebrate the New Year by hunting for a new victim.

The next victim was named Lubie Geter and he had a profile similar to many of the previous victims. Geter was fourteen and spent a lot of time on the streets. He had little adult supervision, spending most of his free time "hustling" for spending money. One of Geter's favorite hustles was selling car deodorizers on street corners and outside convenience stores and supermarkets. On the evening of January 3, he was last seen by his friends talking to a light complexioned black man who was wearing a baseball cap. The man also had a noticeable scar on his face.

Geter's body turned up about a month later in a wooded area along with the bodies of two other boys who had been missing for months.

Although they couldn't do anything to save Lubie Geter, the Task Force believed that his abduction and murder was one of the keys to solving the Atlanta Child Murders case. The description the witness gave of the last person to be with Lubie Geter was considered much more credible than previous descriptions of the supposed killer. However, as credible as the witness was believed to have been and as good as the composite sketch was, it wouldn't do the Task Force any good unless someone came forward.

Although no one came forward to say so, the sketch of Geter's abductor closely resembled Wayne Williams.

The next victim was a fifteen-year-old boy named Terry Pue. Like Geter, Terry Pue ran the streets a lot, doing whatever "hustle" he could to earn a few bucks.

Interestingly, Pue and Geter were also friends, having known each other from the same school and hanging out in the same neighborhood doing the same hustles.

When the Task Force received the report that Terry Pue went missing on January 22, they filed the case as another victim of the Atlanta Child Killer, but their interest was piqued when they learned he was friends with Lubie Geter.

The members of the Task Force believed that the connection was probably not coincidental – the boys must have known their killer.

About a month later Terry Pue's lifeless corpse was pulled from a wooded area about twenty miles from his home. He was later determined to have been strangled to death, like most of the other victims, and was dumped at the location after having been killed.

The discovery of Pue's body also revealed a couple new twists in the investigation. Scratches on Pue's body seemed to indicate that he had fought back against his killer. Although Geter's abduction and murder happened more than two weeks earlier, the investigators immediately took note that witnesses reported the man who was last seen with Geter had a large scar on his face.

The investigators also thought that it was important that Pue's body was discovered more than twenty miles away from his home. The information told the investigators that the killer was somewhat familiar with police procedure and probably dumping the body in a farther away location to confuse them.

The profilers pointed out, though, that it could also be a statement by the killer that he can move around with impunity and that there was little they could do to stop him.

What took place next seems to indicate that killer's reason for dumping Pue's body so far from home was more of the latter than the former.

Beginning in February 1981, the number of victims increased to one a week.

The Task Force realized at that point that the killer was challenging them. He knew that they had no clue about his identity, which gave him the position of power. It was also when

Williams, like all serial killers who have killed many people without getting caught, began to believe that he would never be caught.

"They don't have to worry about inferior police catching them," said FBI profiler Roy Hazelwood about this attitude among serial killers.

Williams, who often refers to himself in third person, simply believed that the Task Force was a bunch of dummies who didn't have what it took to catch Wayne Williams.

So Wayne Williams decided to keep killing and was inadvertently helped by one of the reoccurring conspiracy theories about the case.

"He Got in the Car"

Although few on the Task Force believed that any of the Atlanta Child Murders were committed by Klan, public pressure and a police informant forced them to consider the angle in their investigation.

The more they investigated the Klan, the less likely it seemed that they were involved in any of the crimes. In many ways, though, the Klansmen seemed like the perfect suspects for the crimes. The particular group being investigated was full of avowed white supremacists, many with violent criminal records, who were overheard saying the Atlanta Child Murders were generally a good thing.

As the Task Force zeroed in the small Klan cell in suburban Atlanta, another child was added to the growing list of victims.

Fifteen-year-old Joseph "Jojo" Bell was much like most of the previous victims. He spent a lot of time unsupervised on the streets of Atlanta and especially liked to hang out at a seafood restaurant called "Cap' n Peg's." Bell would sometimes take the trash out, or do other small tasks for the owner, for a little cash or some food from the kitchen.

On the evening of March 2, 1981, Jojo stopped in the restaurant for a few minutes before meeting up with some friends at a nearby basketball court. After the game was over, Jojo was seen getting into a white station wagon with a young light-skinned black man.

Apparently Williams was known to some of the kids playing ball that night because one of them later testified in court about the encounter.

"He got in the car. . . got in Wayne's car," said Jojo's friend.

Besides the witness who claimed to have known Williams, it was also revealed that Williams used the restaurant's address for his band Gemini.

Unfortunately for Jojo, Wayne Williams was far from being on the Task Force's suspect list at that point. In fact, on the night Jojo was abducted the Task Force was conducting surveillance on the Klan lead. Nothing came of the Klan lead but the children of Atlanta kept getting killed.

Less than two weeks after Jojo disappeared, on March 13, thirteen-year-old Timothy Hill disappeared from a neighborhood near downtown. Although Hill and Jojo Bell were separated by two years, which is considerable at that age, they did have a number of things in common. The two boys lived in the same neighborhood and often did the same hustles for cash.

Timothy and Jojo were also friends.

The two boys could often be seen on the streets of Atlanta together, playing basketball and doing odd jobs at Cap' n Peg's restaurant. After Jojo disappeared, Timothy became more cautious on the streets his friends said.

But apparently not cautious enough.

Hill was last seen with some other kids hanging out at a flophouse owned by a convicted sex offender known as "Uncle Tom." When his strangled body was discovered in a wooded area on March 30, the Task Force knew that they had another victim to add to the list.

The Uncle Tom lead was followed up, but it was quickly determined that although the man may have been a sexual deviant, he was not the killer of Atlanta's children.

Wayne Williams just showed up the Task Force, which led to even more public outcry and concern that the killer would never be caught.

More Public Outcry

As the body count tragically increased in early 1981, so too did the public's fear and frustration. Appeals by Atlanta's leaders and the mothers of the victims were slowly but surely being answered by the spring of 1981. The period of the Atlanta Child Murders was long before Facebook and Twitter, or the World Wide Web for that matter, so most people relied on traditional forms of media to get their news.

As news of the Atlanta Child Murders made its way through the newspapers, magazines, and television news programs of America, people with money and power began to take notice.

Former heavyweight boxing legend Muhammad Ali offered to add $500,000 to the existing Task Force reward for any information leading to the arrest of the Atlanta Child killer. The reward garnered a number of tips, none of which led to any arrests, but helped more so by raising the public awareness of the case.

Other notable celebrities of the period who also donated money were Burt Reynolds and Gladys Knight. Most of the money donated by celebrities, as well as the general public, were intended to go toward operating costs of the Task Force or for the victims' families.

Unfortunately, few of the victims' families saw any of the money.

The non-profit organizations that were in charge of the donations were poorly run, which was not entirely their fault. The idea of donating money to support victims of a serial killer was something totally new in the United States so the people running the non-profits were often over their heads concerning logistics.

Around the time that Ali and the other celebrities offered rewards, "Rat Pack" members Sammy Davis Junior and Frank Sinatra gave a concert benefit for the victims' families of the Atlanta Childs Murders. The crooners sang most of their beloved hits and spent ample time between songs speaking to and with the people of Atlanta. Local musicians also performed during the concert and most of the city's leaders were in attendance.

Sinatra and Davis Junior were able to raise quite a sum for the victims' families and bring more awareness to the plight of Atlanta's children, but unfortunately no new tips were raised.

Interestingly, Wayne Williams' father was on stage at the concert in his role as a media photographer.

If only the people of Atlanta knew.

The public pressure that led to the formation of the Task Force also led to President Ronald Reagan publicly acknowledging the Atlanta Child Murders case and assigning his Vice President, George H.W. Bush, to coordinate officially the efforts by local, county, state, and federal law enforcement agencies.

The Task Force was about to massively step up their efforts and pressure.

CHAPTER 6:
The Pressure Builds

The situation of the Atlanta Child Murders case became one where the pressure was beginning to become quite palpable for law enforcement. The citizens' groups that were making their voices heard and the local media's coverage led to national and even international outlets covering the case. The Cable News Network (CNN), which was quite new at the time, assigned some of their top reporters to cover the case and to bring updates to the people of the United States and beyond. Since CNN was based in Atlanta, the studio heads took a particular interest in covering the case.

CNN's coverage of the Atlanta Child Murders had a ripple effect. The more the upstart network covered the case, the more their ratings increased. The Atlanta Child Murders case wasn't the only reason why CNN's ratings surged—the idea of twenty-four-hour television news network was a novelty at the time and drew a number of viewers on that premise alone—but the network set the agenda of the news cycle at the time.

Older, more established media outlets took note and began

covering the case more, which led to more public pressure to solve the murders.

But no matter how much pressure may have been building, there was only so much the Task Force could do.

They couldn't just make up evidence and grab a witness out of thin air.

But members of the Task Force knew that it would only be a matter of time until the killer made a mistake, or for them to discover a mistake he had already made.

A Change in M.O.

When eleven-year-old Patrick Baltazar's body was discovered in early 1981, the investigators knew that the boy's death would be added to the growing list, but they didn't know that he would be the murder that broke the entire case open.

Like most of the other boys who were Wayne Williams' victims, Baltazar was known to hang out on the streets of Atlanta late at night unsupervised. He also did errands and odd jobs for people in his neighborhood, which is what he was doing when he disappeared on the night of February 6, 1981.

When Patrick's body was discovered in a wooded area and when it was determined that he was a young black boy, the Task Force knew that he was another victim in the series so they sent their top forensic crime scene investigators to the scene. The crime scene investigators made sure the scene was uncontaminated and found plenty of physical evidence that was later used against Wayne Williams at trial.

Forensic investigators may not have had the equipment and scientific knowledge available today, but their methods were sound.

Among the physical evidence taken from Patrick Baltazar's body were dog hairs and carpet fibers, which were later determined to match those found on other victims.

The discovery rejuvenated many of the disheartened investigators on the Task Force, who began wondering if they would ever catch the killer.

Unfortunately, though, an overanxious member of the Task Force leaked the information to the media, who then reported the findings in the press.

Just as the Task Force profilers suggested, the killer was intelligent enough to change his tactics. He was also apparently following the case in the media.

The remaining victims' bodies were all dumped in rivers in the Atlanta metropolitan area.

"We concluded from that, that the killer was paying attention to the news reports and thought he was going to, by unclothing the victims, throwing them in the river, that this would cause us not to be able to find the same trace evidence," said Jack Mallard.

Jojo Bell's was the first body to be discovered in a body of water.

Bell's badly decomposed and naked body was found floating in a river in April, several miles away from where he was last seen.

There was also a major change in the victimology from that point forward in the case. Patrick Baltazar was the last pre-teen to be considered a victim of the Atlanta Child Killer. All of the victims immediately after Baltazar were teens and just over a month later all of the victims would be adults.

The Bloody Chattahoochee

Atlanta, Georgia is unique among most American cities in that it is not located on or near a major body of water. As mentioned earlier, the city grew in size because it became a major hub for rail, road, and later air transportation, but it is relatively far from the Atlantic Ocean and not near any major river.

About the closest thing to a major body of water that the Atlanta metropolitan area has is the Chattahoochee River. Although fairly long at 430 miles, the Chattahoochee is not very wide nor deep, so it never became a major transportation route in the era before railroads and automobiles.

Other than some skirmishes during the Civil War, the Chattahoochee's major importance in historical times has been as a recreational hotspot. Canoes, kayakers, hikers and fishermen line the shores of the river on any given day and various points have been popular party spots with young people, as chronicled in the 1993 Alan Jackson hit country music song "Chattahoochee."

But in early 1981 Wayne Williams began using the Chattahoochee as part of his sinister recreational activities.

Beginning in May 1981, six of the last seven victims in the Atlanta Child Murders case were actually adult males between the ages of twenty and twenty-eight. Some who argue that Wayne Williams was not responsible for all, or even most of the Atlanta Child Murders point out that he was only convicted of killing two adult men and that because of that and the fact that most of the last murder victims were actually adults, they were actually two different cases.

But a closer look at some of the last adult victims shows that the change in victims was not actually a total change in victimology.

Although six of the last seven victims were adults, they were all black males and relatively young. All of the men were known to exist on the fringes of society – some had criminal records and all were known to "hustle" for cash, much like their juvenile counterparts on the list of victims.

Some of the adult victims were known to be homosexual or bisexual and none of them were very imposing physically—they tended to be short and slight of build.

Of course, the size of the victims is significant because Wayne Williams only stood 5'6 and was far from athletic. Williams had to use ruses to subdue his victims of equal or smaller stature, and even then there is evidence that some of them put up considerable fights.

The Task Force quickly picked up on the fact that the killer was using the Chattahoochee River as his new dumping ground in an effort to eliminate physical evidence from his victims. Since the river doesn't run through the middle of the city, there are plenty of isolated locations along the river, but near the city, where the killer could've dumped his victims.

But the investigators noted that the bodies were often turning up far from the city, frequently miles to the south.

There are basically only two ways a body can be dumped in a river: it can either be pushed in from shore or dumped from a bridge. The investigators determined that the killer probably wasn't pushing the bodies in the river from shore because they were sometimes found as far as twenty miles from their homes and a body pushed in from shore would likely come back to shore much quicker.

The killer was dumping the body off bridges.

Based on the evidence, the profilers updated their working profile of the Atlanta Child killer. Most of the initial profile still stood, but they added that the killer was either unemployed or worked a night job because he was clearly a night person.

Wayne Williams was a night person.

They also advised the Task Force to watch all bridges in the metro area.

The Stakeout

After Jojo Bell was abducted, murdered, and thrown into a river, the same happened to thirteen-year-old Timothy Hill nearly two weeks later. Then three young adult males – Eddie Duncan, Larry Rogers, and Michael Mcintosh – were all murdered and dumped into a river in less than a one-week period.

But despite knowing what the killer was doing, the Task Force always seemed to be one step behind him.

Wayne Williams was beating the Task Force.

Finally, after two more bodies turned up in the Chattahoochee River in April, the Task Force decided to canvass nearly every bridge in the metro area, which is where profiling once again became important.

Thanks to the efforts of Dettlinger, Hazelwood, and other profilers, the Task Force created a plan whereby they used the killer's M.O. against him. The profilers reported that since the killer had changed his method of dumping bodies from vacant lots to rivers, he would probably continue to do so. If the Task Force wanted to capture the Atlanta Child Killer, then they should focus their efforts on the Chattahoochee River, particularly the bridges, which is where they believed the bodies were being dumped.

With over 100 officers working the case, the Task Force sent teams to stake out previous wooded dump sites, as well as most bridges over the Chattahoochee River in May 1981. This time, though, the Task Force made sure to plug all their leaks so the media wasn't informed of the operation.

The Task Force officers worked long hours for most of the month but turned up few usable leads. A few men were pulled over, but all had credible reasons to be at the place in time and question, or they did not fit the profile.

For some of the top investigators on the Task Force, by the time the end of May was nearing it looked to them as though the serial killer may have moved on, died, or had been arrested on another charge. It had been nearly a month and he hadn't struck, which was a major departure from his one a week pace.

Because of this, the Task Force was about to scale their operations down starting with the stakeouts around Memorial Day 1981.

But then Wayne Williams made his costliest mistake.

Bob Campbell was a young recruit with the Atlanta Police Department who was getting some vital experience working with the Task Force. Although he had seen little action since joining the Task Force, he knew what he was doing was important no matter how difficult or menial the job may have seemed.

Campbell was assigned to do late night-early morning stakeouts of various bridges and wooded areas in the Atlanta area. On the late evening of May 21 and early morning of May 22, he was assigned to a bridge over the Chattahoochee River just to the northwest of Atlanta.

At about 2:30 am, when Campbell was hoping to get a call for a replacement so he could go home and get some sleep, he was startled by a sound in the dark. In fact, there are rumors that he actually was sleeping, which he has consistently denied throughout the years since.

"I was really startled, it sounded " said Campbell when he heard a splash in the river that night. "And I saw break lights . . . the car started moving slowly away from me on the bridge."

Campbell immediately called for back up from Task Force members who were nearby. They pulled over the only car on the road at that hour – a white station wagon driven by a young black male with a light complexion and an afro style haircut.

The young man got out of the car, identified himself as Wayne Williams, and gave his driver's license to the police.

From the beginning, the officers at the scene described Williams as looking agitated and nervous. He kept rubbing his hands and looking around and surprised the officers when he said, "I know this is about those boys."

When asked why he was on the bridge at that hour, Williams told the officers that he was driving to the suburb to Smyrna to check up on a client named Cheryl Johnson. The police later checked the name and address and learned that neither existed.

The police then asked Williams if he turned around on the bridge.

Williams denied stopping and turning around *on* the bridge, saying that he drove across the bridge to call Johnson from a pay phone and when he couldn't get a hold of her he came back and drove over the bridge a second time on his way home.

Interestingly, in more recent interviews, Williams has admitted that the original story he told the police about "Cheryl Johnson" was in fact a lie and that he was simply driving over the bridge to see what activity he could see because he was "just curious as to what I can see in that area."

Although the stakeouts weren't widely reported, Williams did have access to police scanners and radios, which brings up an interesting question: should Williams then have known that stakeouts were being conducted on the bridges? It would seem that either Williams failed to check his police radio, the Task Force maintained radio silence or used code, or that he just didn't care.

After all, in Wayne Williams' mind he was smarter than the Task Force.

As the police were questioning Williams on the bridge, more than one officer noticed that he fit the composite sketch drawn from the eyewitness who last seen with Lubbie Geter. Williams allowed the police to search his car, but they only found a nylon cord, which for some reason they didn't confiscate.

Although Wayne Williams certainly looked and acted suspiciously on the bridge that night, the Task Force didn't have any evidence to arrest him. They let Williams drive home that night, but made sure to let him know that they would be watching him.

On the evening Williams was pulled over, twenty-seven-year-old Nathaniel Cater was last seen alive. His partially decomposed body was discovered three days later in the Chattahoochee River not far from the bridge where Wayne Williams was stopped.

The coroner ruled that Cater was probably strangled to death and although there were no traces of bodily fluids found on his body, the investigators believed that the murder was sexual in nature.

The profilers on the Task Force argued that although there was a practical reason to strip the bodies, it was also part of the killer's signature. Removing the clothes was part of the killer's ritual and was probably part of a sexual act whereby the killer never actually sexually penetrated the victim's body.

It was also quickly added to the list of other Atlanta Child Murders victims, although Cater was an adult.

Despite his age, Cater fit the profile of most of the other victims. He was a relatively young black male and was actually slight of build. Williams could've overpowered Cater with the right ruse. Cater also lived on the edge of society like many of the younger victims. He was a convicted felon who committed petty crimes and "hustles" just to get by and was also known to engage in homosexual activity for money and pleasure.

Nathaniel Cater is the last known victim in the series.

Wayne Williams VS the Task Force

After Nathaniel Cater's body was discovered on the banks of the Chattahoochee River, the Task Force knew that Wayne Williams was their man. Not all of the investigators believed that he was responsible for all twenty-eight of the murders on the list, but most thought that he committed a majority of the killings.

The Task Force was in agreement that Williams had to be stopped.

The initial circumstantial evidence certainly didn't look good for Williams: he was stopped where a body was later found, an officer heard a splash before he was pulled over, he acted and looked suspicious, and none of the answers he gave to the police officers added up.

But none of that was enough to make an arrest, never mind bring Williams to trial.

So immediately after Williams was pulled over on the bridge, the Task Force set about to learn more about their prime suspect. The Task Force had kept a lengthy file of potential suspects throughout their investigation, which they reduced and added to as they interviewed and investigated the suspects.

Wayne Williams was not on their suspect list.

Investigators first conducted a thorough background check of Williams before reinitiating contact with him. The Task Force interviewed friends, former classmates, and business associates of the man whom they believed was the Atlanta Child Murderer, often hearing many of the same things. Wayne was a smart, fairly ambitious guy who was usually helpful and conscientious. The profilers were not surprised to hear these sorts of things; after all, they knew that the killer would possess an average to above average IQ, and he would be able to blend in among the crowd.

The fact that Williams was known to be friendly and helpful also didn't surprise the profilers. Most serial killers can put on a "normal" public façade that allows them to avoid suspicion, sometimes for years. In this respect Wayne Williams was no different than any other serial killer.

The Task Force also learned that Williams was a loner.

He had no real close friends and wasn't known to date women or men. Clearly, many parts of Wayne Williams' life remained a mystery to most.

Wayne Williams fit the profile of the Atlanta Child Murderer.

Although the Task Force was unanimous in their conviction that Wayne Williams murdered Nathanial Cater and most were also convinced he killed most, if not all, of the other Atlanta Child Murders victims, they didn't even have enough evidence to get a search warrant for his home or car.

The profilers knew, though, that they could appeal to Williams' ego.

Like many serial killers, the profilers believed that Williams wouldn't avoid an opportunity to show that he was smarter than the police.

And to throw them off his scent.

The Task Force contacted Williams and requested him to come into the Atlanta Police Department headquarters for an interview on June 3, 1981. They told him that it was merely routine since he was stopped near the location of where a body was found and that if he answered some simple questions then they could take him off their list.

No doubt Williams looked at the interview as a challenge. It was all part of an elaborate cat and mouse game to Wayne Williams, but in his egotistical mind he believed he was the cat when in reality he was the mouse.

The Task Force interviewed, or more like interrogated, Williams for several hours that evening, but he never admitted to committing any murder.

Williams was then asked if he would take a polygraph exam.

He agreed to take the exam, which he promptly failed. The Task Force then gave him the chance to take the exam twice more, but he failed both of those exams.

Richard Radcliff, who was the FBI polygraph examiner who gave Williams the test later recalled how he looked at Williams and said, "I'll be darned, you're the guy we've been looking for, for two years."

Polygraph exam results are not admissible in any American courtroom and a failed exam is not even enough to make an arrest, so Williams was allowed to go home early in the morning.

The media learned of the interview but were not given Williams' name or address.

The Task Force knew they had the right man and they let Wayne Williams know it.

It was now time for Williams to make a move.

Cleaning Up

Although the media had yet to announce Wayne Williams as the Task Force's prime suspect in the Atlanta Child Murders case, the news spread quickly in the Williams' neighborhood that Wayne had been brought in for questioning. The neighbors began paying attention more closely to the activities in and around the Williams home and noticed that in the days immediately after June 3 there was more movement than what was normal.

Witnesses reported Wayne Williams and his father doing extensive cleaning on the outside of the home and in the yard in the days after the bridge incident. They were seen mowing the lawn, raking the yard, and cleaning the windows, which in itself is not very strange, but they seemed to take extra time to do the normally mundane tasks.

Wayne also took several hours to clean out his white station wagon.

After Wayne and his father were done cleaning the yard and car, they apparently cleaned most of the inside of the house.

The neighbors saw Wayne and his father carry several boxes to the station wagon and then drive away for several hours.

The two were then seen on another day burning various items in their outdoor grill. Due to the smell of the smoke, it was clear to the neighbors that they weren't burning wood or charcoal.

The normally friendly Williams family was also curt towards their neighbors during this period. When neighbors asked what they were doing, Wayne and his father simply ignored them and went about their business of cleaning and burning.

Everything seemed so strange and out of place to the Williams' neighbors.

When the Task Force learned that Wayne Williams and his father were potentially destroying evidence related to the Atlanta Child Murders case, they moved quickly to get a search warrant for the Williams home. In the application for the warrant, the investigators argued that Williams behavior on the bridge combined with his failing three polygraph exams and his recent activities around his home called for a search warrant.

The judge agreed and issued a search warrant for the Williams home and all their cars.

The Task Force spent the better part of a day carefully sifting through every inch of the Williams home and cars. They paid particular attention to all the carpets and rugs in the home and cars. The forensic examiners also noticed that the Williams family had a pet German Shepherd, so they took some hairs from it.

With so much activity around the case, it was becoming increasingly difficult for the Task Force to keep the developments from the media so they decided to issue a statement.

But the statement proved to be a bit strange and not what all investigators believed. The statement was given by Atlanta Public Safety Commissioner Lee Brown, who stated that he believed there was still more than one killer on the prowl.

"It has consistently been our position based upon the evidence that we do not have a single person that has involved in the cases involved with the children. That is our position today we know based upon the evidence. And we're looking at the data we have at our disposal. We're looking at things such as modus operandi that is how people commit crimes. And based upon all of that using our own experience in the field of law enforcement. The experience and opinions of those who have consulted with us including law enforcement agencies, our consultants etc. We can say with certainty that we do not have one person responsible for the cases involving the missing and murdered children in our city," said Brown.

Regardless of how many people some on the Task Force believed were involved in the Atlanta Child Murders case, all knew that Wayne Williams was somehow involved.

And they were building a strong case against him.

The Developing Case Against Wayne Williams

As Wayne Williams remained free during the first few weeks of June 1981, the Task Force set about to build their legal case against him. They had determined that he was definitely responsible for Cater's murder, and despite Lee Brown's statement, most believed that he was good for the majority of the child murders.

Although 1981 may not be that long ago relatively speaking, it was in terms of forensic science.

The process of DNA profiling, which has become a ubiquitous part of most murder investigations today, was still about seven years in the future.

Another aspect of criminology that is often taken granted for today, but which was much less prevalent in 1981 is the presence of closed-circuit cameras. Today, most private businesses, especially in major cities, usually have at least one camera to ward off criminals and record any wrongdoing. Due to the increasingly low prices of security cameras and the ease by which one can install and run them through home computers, many individuals also have security cameras in and around their homes.

Security cameras were still rare in 1981,

Although closed-circuit television became cheaper and easier to use by the late 1970s due to the advent of video tape recorders, it was still rare to see businesses with them during Wayne Williams' murder spree. Closed-circuit television cameras were still the preview of government installations and big businesses at that time, unlike today where many homes have cost-efficient security camera systems.

Still, some of the businesses in downtown Atlanta had closed-circuit television cameras

Wayne Williams was never known to have been captured on one.

Still, the Task Force had managed to compile a mountain of circumstantial and physical evidence against Wayne Williams.

In today's world where both true crime and fictional television shows about forensic science are common, many people are skeptical about the use of circumstantial evidence against a criminal defendant. The reality is that people are routinely convicted of crimes based on circumstantial evidence alone. Of course, the circumstantial evidence used to convict a person of a crime usually has to be quite damning and there is often quite a bit.

There was a decent sized hill of circumstantial evidence that pointed toward Wayne Williams' guilt in early June 1981, and it kept growing every day.

Besides the astronomical coincidence that Williams just happened to be on a bridge at the time a splash was heard, and where the body of the last victim was recovered days later, his behavior during the subsequent encounter with the police did not scream "innocent."

Then there was the fact that Williams had no credible alibi for any of the murders. During the all-night interrogation on June 3, Williams told the investigators that he was out either doing his freelance journalist or talent scout work when asked about his location when several of the victims went missing, although he was never clear about dates or times.

Wayne Williams couldn't provide the names of anyone who could corroborate his alibis.

Williams was also connected to more than one victim.

As mentioned earlier, he used the seafood restaurant where Jojo Bell hung out as a mailing address and was known by some of Bell's friends.

He also closely matched the composite sketch of Bell's abductor.

And Williams was reported to have had several scratches on his face, much like what witnesses said Bell's abductor had.

People who worked with Williams in the music industry told investigators that he often had scratches on his face and arms during the height of the Atlanta Child Murders case.

A woman named Kathy Andrews who worked with Williams in the early 1980s recalled on a particularly troubling incident.

"At one point in time when Wayne came for one of the sessions he walked into the back of the studio and he had horrible scratches on his arm."

Williams told her that he fell in a bush, but there were far too many wounds and they were much too deep to be from a simple roll through a briar patch.

Andrews became afraid of Williams and avoided him at that point.

Williams was also said to have been connected to twenty-year-old victim Larry Rogers. According to Rogers' mother, Wayne Williams once hid Larry's younger brother from the police and drove him to the hospital after he was injured in a fight.

As bad as the circumstantial evidence may have been, it was bolstered by a host of physical evidence.

Although the case against Wayne Williams took place years before the advent of DNA profiling, blood and hair evidence could still be used as evidence. Blood found in Williams' car and at his home could be matched with type. Obviously, such analysis could only narrow things down, but combined with other physical and circumstantial evidence it could be damning.

The same was true for hairs found on the victims or in Williams' car and home, including dog hairs. Of course none of this could prove anything with certainty, but when combined with other physical and circumstantial evidence they could be another nail in Williams' legal coffin.

But what would prove to be the key piece of physical evidence used against Wayne Williams was the carpet fiber evidence.

While Wayne Williams was free for most of June 1981, Larry Peterson and the other forensic analysists were looking at every carpet, rug, and blanket taken from the Williams home and Wayne's white station wagon. The fiber found on Eric Middlebrook's was matched to a rug from the Williams home.

"The shape was the most distinctive feature of the fiber," Peterson said in an interview years later.

The fiber in question was a distinctive trilobal fiber, which although not unique, offered a solid forensic starting point in the investigation. Like the blood and hair evidence, the fibers could help to narrow down the suspect pool.

Peterson had been working with that fiber for nearly two years so he knew it like the back of the hand. When he was asked how quickly he knew that the fiber from Middlebrooks and the rug were made of the same material, he answered.

"I knew instantly it was."

Peterson was assisted by Hal Deadman, who was the FBI's top microanalyst at the time.

"My initial role was to assist the Georgia crime laboratory in attempting to identify these fibers. To see if the manufacturer of these fibers could be identified," said Deadman.

Deadman's assistance proved to be a boon to the investigation. Although Peterson and the other GBI investigators were qualified and competent professionals, their office had limited resources. Once the FBI came on board, they received nearly unlimited resources, which later proved to be vital when they matched the fibers to its ultimate source and manufacturer.

In the month between the bridge incident and Wayne William's ultimate arrest in late June, Deadman worked long hours to locate the manufacturer and retailer of the carpet. Until he could definitively do that, Williams remained free.

The Press Conference

A press conference is a standard way for people or organizations to convey their messages to the public via the media. Generally speaking, press conferences are supposed to be exercises of transparency where the people giving the conference "lay all their cards on the table," so to speak.

Most people who do the speaking at press conferences are seasoned professionals who have been trained to deal with the media and are often former members of the media themselves. The primary reason for this is because the press is traditionally allowed to ask questions, which can create problems if the person giving the conference is not a professional and/or hasn't been properly prepared.

Needless to say, criminals don't usually do well in press conferences.

Someone without a background in public speaking or media relations will usually be exposed if they lie during a press conference and suspicious behavior or activities are usually amplified.

But to a narcissist with delusions of grandeur, a press conference is the perfect place to show the world how right he is.

No matter if he is wrong.

Megalomania, hubris, and delusions of grandeur were all driving forces in the life of Wayne Williams, so when the Task Force conducted a search warrant at his parents' home, he believed that only he could set everyone straight.

The day after the Task Force searched the Williams home and took away boxes of physical evidence, Wayne Williams gave a press conference bright and early at seven am in his parents' home. Like a typical sociopath, Williams had to be in control, which is why he did the conference at his home. No doubt Williams believed that the familiar environment would make him more comfortable when he answered questions that could decide the rest of his life. Having the press conference in a typical middle-class American home was potentially good optics as well.

Before the details of the press conference were finalized, Williams made the press agree to a couple of other demands.

He stipulated that the camera never show his face during the press conference and for his name not to be released.

The press agreed to all of Wayne Williams' demands.

It may seem strange today, in the world of routine press leaks, that the media would agree to such demands, but it was a different time in the country and the members of the press were chasing the biggest story of their careers.

They were willing to play along with the Atlanta Child Murders suspect for the time being.

Even without the stipulations, the press conference would've been bizarre to say the least. There are no other known examples of suspected serial killers giving press conferences and the fact that he did so in his own home gave it a surreal feel.

When the press asked Williams about the victims, his reply was particularly glib and lacking in any sort of empathy.

"Some of these kids in places they don't have no business being at certain times of the day and night, some of them don't have no kind of home supervision and they're just running around in the streets wild. And I'm saying, when you're doing that, that's not giving anyone a license to kill, but you're opening yourself up for all kinds of things," said Williams.

The members of the press looked both disturbed and in awe by Williams' strange answer, but pressed on with more questions.

For his part, Williams sounded relaxed, comfortable, and in his element. He was after all the master of ceremonies in a production that he had been conducting for nearly two years. He also had high verbal skills and a background in media, which he seemed to employ quite well during his monologue and the question and answer portion of the press conference.

After showing little regard for the victims, Williams then shifted to the Task Force, directing most of his vitriol toward the officers and their efforts. To Wayne Williams, he was the victim, which the people of America needed to know.

Williams next claimed that the Task Force had it out for him personally and implied that if he were arrested, it would only be because the investigators were tired of the case and that he was an easy target.

"One of the Task Force captains on the scene pointed his finger at me and said it that he was tired of all the BS about working the long hours, working the stakeouts and that he was ready to pull the thing to an end," said Williams.

Wayne was right, though, that the Task Force was about to "pull the thing to an end," although not in the way he wanted.

Williams ended the press conference by berating the Task Force some more and bringing everything back to himself. After all, in Wayne Williams' mind he was the true victim in this situation. He passed plenty of blame around – the police were generally incompetent and possibly devious in their targeting of him and the media was also to blame. Williams lectured the media on how to better do their jobs, suggesting that due to his experience in the field he was an expert on the matter.

Although Williams' face was not visible during the press conference, due to the statements he made and the tone of his voice, it was clear that he probably had quite the defiant and arrogant look on his face. For their part, the members of the media looked intrigued and at times perplexed by what the prime and only suspect in the Atlanta Child Murders case was saying to them.

Williams finally ended the press conference by doing what any other narcissistic serial killer would do in his situation – ask for an apology.

"I'm asking for a public apology from the FBI or whoever was responsible for leaking this information to the news media," said Williams.

Wayne Williams would have to wait a long time for that apology.

Cat and Mouse

One trait that all narcissists have in common, serial killer or not, is that they all want to be the center of attention. Narcissists are willing to push the envelope of what is considered acceptable behavior in order to have their face seen or to have their name said.

Serial killer narcissists display these traits even more so than the average narcissist.

Some serial killers like to taunt the police during their reigns of terror, while others eat up the attention during their trials. And some, such as Ted Bundy, seem to do both.

Since Williams had a media background, it is likely that he followed his deeds on the local news and in the newspapers, which would've given him a thrill.

But Wayne Williams' ego seemed to be driven more by a need to dominate others. For Williams, the thrill of the hunt and his supposed ability to fool law enforcement is what drove his narcissistic impulses.

Although the press agreed not to show Williams' face or say his name during the press conference, the agreement apparently didn't extend after the conference. Williams' name and address, along with numerous pictures of him, were broadcast by news outlets around the world as the prime suspect in the Atlanta Child Murders case.

Suddenly, the Williams home became ground zero in a media circus.

Reporters and cameramen from media outlets from around the country, and a few from Europe, were camped out on the street in front of the home day and night. The spectacle and news of the suspect then drew countless gawkers, who drove by the Williams home in a seemingly endless stream to see where the only suspect in the Atlanta Child Murders case lived.

The Task Force was there too.

Although the profilers on the Task Force didn't think Williams would try to run because he would feel the need to "prove" his innocence, the media attention presented several intangibles that were difficult to control. The possibility existed that an angry member of one of the victims' families may try to exact revenge, or even a vigilante with an inflated sense of justice would try to do his good deed by killing Williams.

It was also becoming apparent that Wayne and his father were getting quite upset with the gawkers who drive by their home and the impromptu media camp. They reasoned that either man could violently lash out in frustration at a reporter or bystander.

There was also the possibility that Williams would be so arrogant that he would try to claim another victim right under the Task Force's nose.

In order to mitigate some of these potential problems, the Task Force decided to place a LoJack type device on Williams' car in order to track his movements. The technology was relatively new in 1981 and required a receiver to be within relatively close proximity, but it proved to be useful when Williams left home a number of times abruptly.

For seventeen days after he gave his press conference, Wayne Williams was relentlessly hounded by both the media and the Task Force.

And it became clear quite early that the pressure was starting to have an effect.

Wayne and his father would routinely emerge from their home to tell the press to stay off their lawn and Wayne would occasionally work his way through the throng to leave in his white station wagon.

Williams threatened to take the press and the Task Force to court for harassment, but nothing came of the threats.

He would sometimes leave in the middle of the night and drive around the city aimlessly. Members of the Task Force looked at these late night jaunts with mixed emotions. On the one hand they were afraid that he was going to add another victim to the list of twenty-eight victims, but on the other hand they almost hoped he would try it. The Task Force would almost surely be able to stop any attempted abduction and if they did then they would have him dead to rights.

But nothing in life is certain and things can always go wrong.

On one occasion he even stopped in front of the mayor's home and made a scene. On other occasions he engaged in high-speed cat and mouse games with the Task Force.

Williams later justified his behavior.

"When you're trying to get into your own home and you have to literally fight your way through a sea of people . . . it was frustrating," recalled Williams.

As frustrating as Williams claimed the situation was for him, it was even more so for the people of Atlanta and the Task Force, who wanted to see the Atlanta Child Murders case closed. Working with the district attorney, the investigators wanted to build an airtight case against Williams that would hold up in a trial and on appeal. They knew they really only had one chance to get Williams, so they waited to make their move until they had all their "t's" crossed and all their "i's" dotted.

Once that was done, the Task Force made its move on June 21, 1981.

CHAPTER 7:
The Trial of Wayne Williams

In general, arrests for major crimes are often complicated procedures, but the situation is made even more so when the case is a high profile one such as the Atlanta Child Murders. In cases such as these, the investigators only make arrests when they know they have enough evidence and often work closely with the district attorney or county prosecutor.

It is the prosecutor's job to ensure that the case against a defendant is strong enough for a conviction.

Because of that, prosecutors often undercharge a defendant, only charging the person with crimes where they are nearly positive they can win a conviction.

In the Atlanta Child Murders case, it was perhaps a bit ironic that the two murders where the prosecutors believed they had the best chance to convict Williams on were actually adults—Nathaniel Cater and twenty-one-year-old Jimmy Payne, who went missing on April 23, 1981.

Still, prosecutor Jack Mallard and most of the members of the Task Force were convinced Williams was good for all, or most, of the murders on the list. They reasoned that if convicting Williams of any murder was good because it would get him off the streets permanently.

The Arrest

Once the Fulton County prosecutor's office decided to go ahead with two first-degree murder charges against Wayne Williams, the Task Force had to develop a plan to extract him from his parent's home with as little resistance and fanfare as possible.

Although the profilers didn't believe that Williams would put up an armed struggle or attempt to take his own life, they could never be too sure. The Task Force also wanted to take Williams in front of as few cameras as possible.

In the early morning hours of June 21, 1983, the Task Force descended on the Williams home and took Wayne Williams with no resistance.

Williams was described as looking disheveled and confused. Others said he looked defeated.

Williams was quickly arraigned in Fulton County court and denied bail. He would have to sit in isolation in the county jail for nearly six months before his trial began on January 6, 1982.

The trial of Wayne Williams actually progressed much quicker than most murder trials do today. It is not uncommon in most jurisdictions today for defendants facing first-degree murder charges to sit in the county jail a year to three years before going to trial, but everything moved faster in Williams' trial.

Much of that had to do with the fact that Williams' attorneys were unseasoned in murder trials and simply didn't file many pre-trial motions or briefs. They let the pre-trial hearings proceed with few objections and they had little money to hire experts and investigators, which also could lead to trial delays.

With that said, Williams still had to sit in the county jail for half a year.

And he wasn't allowed into the general population.

As soon as the Task Force made Williams their only suspect in early June, the Fulton County Sheriff's Office began building a special wing of the Fulton County Jail. The wing was basically an isolated section of the jail that was meant to house only one person – the Atlanta Child Murders suspect. The purpose of the wing was to prevent Williams from escaping, but also to prevent other inmates from killing him.

The special block also served to keep Williams from killing himself.

There were rumors that several people had put a "hit" out on Williams and any inmate who wanted to make a name for himself could have done so by attacking him. The authorities didn't want to be responsible for the death of one of America's most hated men and possibly give more fuel to conspiracy theories.

Wayne Williams needed to go to trial for all to see.

So Williams spent his days alone, with the exception of visits from his lawyers, under twenty-four-hour observation. He was allowed out for exercise once a day by himself, but never came into contact with other inmates.

As Williams sat in isolation and his lawyers prepared for his trial, the atmosphere outside was charged and tense. Media outlets from every region of the United States and several from outside the country converged on downtown Atlanta to cover the trial. It proved to be one of the first major serial killer trials to be covered extensively by the media, which didn't disappoint as they reported every salacious detail they could from the case.

One of the first major pre-trial battles that many thought Williams lawyers would fight would be a change of venue for the trial. It is common in high-profile trials for defense lawyers to attempt to change the location of the trial due to what is perceived as bias in the jurisdiction where the defendant has been charged.

Williams' lawyers publicly stated that they believed their defendant could get a fair trial in Fulton County. Wayne Williams would face a jury of his true peers—men and women from his hometown. Williams' legal team also believed that they had a better chance with a jury from predominantly black Atlanta than in other parts of the state that were less black and more rural and/or suburban.

Since the Atlanta Child Murders case was racially charged almost from the beginning due to several conspiracy theories, the prosecution had to consciously avoid anything that may have made them look bias during jury selection. For the most part, though, Mallard and the prosecution team wasn't worried that a predominantly black jury would acquit Williams for purely racial reasons.

All his victims were black and they only needed to seat jurors who were hardworking and believed in law and order, which was not difficult in a county the size of Fulton.

In the end, the jury was comprised of eight black and four whites, nine women and three men.

Due to the high-profile nature of the trial, it was decided that the jury would be sequestered and their access to the media would be highly restricted. Although the sequestration was bothersome because the trial lasted eight weeks, the jurors took their duty in stride with there being few complaints.

The choice of the trial judge also proved to be an aspect of the case that was somewhat controversial.

Fulton County officials announced that the judge would be picked randomly through a computer program, which seemed fair to both the prosecution and defense, but when the judge's name was announced the choice didn't appear very random.

Judge Clarence Cooper was announced as the trial judge. By all accounts, Judge Cooper had an impressive resume and to most familiar with him he was viewed as fair and impartial. To those a little more cynical, though, Judge Cooper looked like the perfect choice for the prosecution.

Cooper was the first black judge elected to the Fulton County bench, which immediately allayed fears among many that he would be racially biased against Williams. But a deeper look into Cooper's background revealed that he was a former prosecutor who served alongside District Attorney Jack Slaton for many years.

Some thought that the move stacked the deck against Williams.

Others believed that Williams had stacked the deck against himself.

The Prosecution's Case

The Fulton County prosecutors believed that their case against Williams was airtight because it was built on a mountain of physical evidence, with a fair amount of corroborating circumstantial evidence. Instead of leaking their evidence against Williams to the press before the trial, the prosecution for the most part stayed tight-lipped, preferring to try the case in the courtroom.

The media had already learned about some of the carpet evidence, but the trial would reveal a lot more.

Still, there was the question that persisted in the media and among the public in general: what drove Wayne Williams to kill so many children?

This is a question that has been asked of nearly every known serial killer in history and has usually been answered inadequately at best. Williams bizarre behavior before the killings was known, but it still didn't provide a motive for so many murders and although the prosecution is not required to prove a motive to get a conviction – only that the defendant's guilt is beyond reasonable doubt – it certainly helps in most cases.

In the case against Williams, the profilers were consulted once more to establish a motive.

A large part of profiling a killer also involves assembling a profile of the killer's victims, or what is known as "victimology." In the Atlanta Child Murders case, all of the victims were black, nearly all were male, and all were under the age of thirty. Although most serial killers kill within their own race, the profilers thought that there was something more going on in this case.

They believed that Wayne Williams had an animus toward members of his own race.

They based this theory on statements Williams made over the years combined with the fact that most of the murders were done very intimately, literally "hands on."

The profilers also believed that there was a sexual component to the murders.

Although there was never semen recovered on or in any of the victims, the profilers believed that the crimes were committed out of a sense of sexual frustration. The fact that many of the bodies were discovered nude, even before Williams began dumping the victims in rivers, also seemed to indicate that the killer was getting sexually aroused by the entire process.

Based on the profilers' examinations, the prosecution argued that Wayne Williams was driven to kill out of a combination of hatred for his race and repressed homosexuality.

Still, the prosecutors knew that the crux of their case against Williams would be the physical evidence.

Although Williams was only charged with two of the murders, the presiding judge allowed physical evidence from the other Atlanta Child Murders case to be used in court.

And the evidence proved to be extremely damning.

Nineteen different carpet fibers taken from Williams' white station wagon were matched to those found on twelve of the twenty-eight victims attributed to the Atlanta Child Murderer. The prosecution was positive that the fibers were a match and proved that Wayne Williams was the elusive serial killer, but they still had to prove that to a jury of ordinary men and women who had no background in forensic science.

In other words, the evidence against Williams needed to be presented by Mallard and the prosecution in a way that the jury would understand. Technical jargon needed to be avoided in favor of "down home" language, which happened to be Mallard's specialty,

The prosecution's forensic experts testified how the yellowish-green fibers found on the victims were determined to have been manufactured by the Wellman Corporation and that after contacting the company they were able to narrow things down even more.

The experts learned that the fibers were from a specific carpet that was manufactured in Dalton, Georgia from 1967 to 1974.

The Task Force then examined all sales records of that type of carpet and ultimately established that there was only a 1 in 7,792 chance of finding a similar carpet in the Atlanta metropolitan area.

Skeptics reading this will immediately point out that based on those numbers there were certainly others, perhaps as many as a few hundred, in the Atlanta area who had the same carpet.

But there were few others in the Atlanta area, if any, who had the same carpet as well as other physical and circumstantial evidence that tied them to the murders.

Hair and blood evidence was also introduced by the prosecution that potentially connected Williams to several of the victims. Although DNA profiling was not available at the time to definitely link Williams to the victims, blood typing could narrow things down and similar analysis could be made with hair.

A dog hair found on Nathanial Cater's body was consistent with a German Shepard. The Williams family owned a German Shepard at the time.

Also, human hairs consistent with Williams' were discovered on the inside of Patrick Baltazar's shirt.

Finally, blood taken from the interior of Wayne Williams' white station wagon was matched to the same type as multiple Atlanta Child Murders victims.

As damaging as the physical evidence was against Williams, a plethora of circumstantial evidence proved to be the final nail in his legal coffin.

Williams' strange and creepy behavior before the killings came back to hurt him during the trial as there was no shortage of witnesses who were willing to take the stand against him. Although none of the witnesses who testified against Williams claimed to have seen him assault any of the victims, some placed him with victims just before their disappearances.

For Williams' part, he later claimed that all of the witnesses were lying, but there were just so many who testified that it is difficult to believe that they all lied.

And why would they lie?

A kid named Eugene Lester, who was a friend of Jojo Bell and was playing basketball with him the night he disappeared, identified Williams in court as the man who was driving the white station wagon that Bell was seen getting into.

A number of other witnesses were called who testified that Williams was a homosexual with pedophile tendencies. One of these witnesses claimed that Williams once told her that he "could knock out black street kids in a few minutes by putting his hand on their necks."

Perhaps one of the most damning eyewitnesses to testify was a young man named Robert Henry. Henry was certainly no angel and far from a perfect witness. Like many of the victims, Henry was a bit of a street hustler and a small-time crook with a criminal record. He definitely had several skeletons in his closet that the defense tried to take advantage of during cross-examination. Henry was also not very educated, didn't speak well, and wasn't very bright. He was certainly the type of witness that would be called last to testify, but he had an air of honesty about him.

He also knew Nathanial Cater through work and claimed to have seen him with Wayne Williams the night he disappeared.

"They were holding hands, you know, like male and female," said Henry. "If you're holding hands with one of my coworkers and both you are male, what am I supposed to do, turn my head?"

Henry didn't turn his head and testified in court that he was positive it was Wayne Williams with Nathanial Cater that night. He was vigorously cross-examined by Williams' attorneys, but stuck to his story.

The jury saw Robert Henry as a credible witness.

Cater was known to be bisexual and would sometimes prostitute himself out to men to supplement his meager income. One of the places that Cater was known to frequent was a gay bar popular with black men in the downtown area known as the Silver Dollar. Regulars and employees of the bar testified that Cater was a regular and that Wayne Williams visited the establishment on more than one occasion as well.

The combination of physical and circumstantial evidence against Wayne Williams was obviously a major, if not impossible, obstacle for the defense to overcome, but it was only made so because the judge allowed evidence of other murders Williams wasn't charged with to be used as evidence. The presiding judge allowed the prosecution to use physical evidence taken from the scene of ten other murders from the Atlanta Child Murders case to prove a pattern.

These other murders became known as the "pattern" cases or "pattern murders."

Although it may seem controversial for a judge to allow evidence from crimes a defendant has not been charged with to be used against the defendant, it is not unusual in American courtrooms. The state of Georgia allowed for the use of "pattern" evidence before Williams' trial and other states have and still allow similar evidence.

Much of the fiber and hair evidence used against Williams actually came from some of these other murders for which he was never charged. The ten victims allowed in as pattern evidence included the first victims, Alfred Evans, and Eric Middlebrooks, on whose shoe the first carpet fiber was discovered.

Other victims who were allowed as pattern evidence included twelve-year-old Charles Stephens, who disappeared on October 9, 1980 and was later determined to have been suffocated once his body was discovered.

Fifteen-year-old Terry Pue, who disappeared on January 22, 1981, was discovered strangled to death weeks later.

The oldest victim on the list, twenty-eight-year-old John Porter, who was stabbed to death in April 1981, was also allowed to be used as pattern evidence.

Lubie Geter, Jojo Bell, and Patrick Baltazar, who were all found with physical evidence that incriminated Williams, or who were connected to him in some way, were also referenced by the prosecution.

Another one of the adult victims, twenty-year-old Larry Rogers, was on the list. One of the last victims, seventeen-year-old William Barrett, who disappeared on May 11, 1981, and was later discovered strangled to death, rounded out the list of pattern murders that the prosecution were allowed to use.

Besides some of the pattern victims having been discovered with incriminating physical evidence on them, or having some connection to Wayne Williams, the prosecution argued that all the victims fit a specific profile or victimology. They further argued that the victimology in the case helped prove Williams' motive, as well as demonstrating his twisted but sane state of mind.

The characteristics of the pattern were outlined by the prosecution in their opening arguments.

The most obvious characteristic of the pattern was that all victims were black males. Most of the victims were also children, but even the adults were young, with the oldest being the relatively young age of twenty-eight.

Although some of juvenile victims were quite fit and athletic for their ages, the adults were typically short with small builds, which placed the average size of the victims below 5'6 and under 150 pounds.

In other words, nearly all victims were either Wayne Williams' size or smaller.

Nearly all of the victims were discovered nude. Although it was determined that a major reason why many of the victims were discovered nude, especially the later victims, was because Williams attempted to eliminate physical evidence, the profilers on the Task Force believed that it was also part of the killer's signature. The nude bodies represented a form of sexual dominance and possibly the fact that the killer had some type of sexual activity with or near the bodies before dumping them.

The fact that none of the ten victims on the pattern list owned a car was deemed significant. The prosecution argued that Williams, like all serial killers, preyed on people's weaknesses and vulnerabilities and that his ability to offer rides played a key role in his M.O. and was a unique aspect of his victims' backgrounds.

The prosecutors also argued that other key aspects of Williams' M.O. could be discerned in the so-called pattern murders. The fact that nearly every victim was murdered in one location and then transported to another dump site was significant.

The dump sites were also a significant part of Williams' M.O. and said a lot about his state of mind.

All dump sites were either wooded areas or rivers. Although they were often somewhat isolated locations, they were still located within the metropolitan area and were also close to densely populated neighborhoods. The dump sites were obviously practical in nature, but the prosecution also argued that only someone who could move effortlessly in these neighborhoods could access these spots on numerous occasions.

They argued that the killer had to be someone who was extremely mobile and well-acquainted with every part of the city, even its darkest corners. The killer would therefore either be unemployed or have a job where he could travel a lot within the metropolitan area.

Wayne Williams fit that description perfectly.

The prosecution also believed that the lifestyles of the victims was a key characteristic in the pattern.

All of the victims spent considerable time on the streets of Atlanta. Most of the juvenile victims were involved in hustles such as running errands and doing odd jobs around their neighborhoods for money, while the adult victims were often connected to petty crime and homosexual prostitution.

The fact that the method of disposal of the victims and the victims' ages changed in 1981, did not present any problems the prosecution argued. When Williams switched from dumping his victims in vacant lots or rivers just showed that his criminal sophistication was growing as he killed—he was learning as he killed.

And the fact that his later victims were a bit older was for the most part due to availability. The combination of media pressure, community involvement, and curfews limited the number of juveniles Williams had access to, so he had to modify his victimology slightly.

Again, although the later victims were all adults, the prosecution pointed out, they didn't deviate much from the victimology of the earlier victims.

Finally, the victims in the pattern murders all had either the fibers from rugs and carpets from the Williams home on them, or hairs that were similar to those from Wayne Williams or his dog. The blood taken from Williams' car was also matched in type to more than one of the pattern murders.

The case against Wayne Williams was truly monumental, but it was not airtight.

The Defense

In the United States, defense attorneys have the responsibility to put on the best defense for their clients that the law and resources allow. The key is the term "resources," which of course means money and therefore the ability to hire experts. A defendant with a lot of money is able to hire high-profile attorneys, who in turn can hire world-renowned experts to counter the prosecution's expert witnesses.

Or a wealthy defendant's lawyers can simply put on a better show and/or call witnesses that can confuse the jury and obfuscate the prosecution's case.

When O.J. Simpson was on trial in 1995 for the murder of his ex-wife, he hired a "dream team" of high-profile attorneys, who put countless witnesses on the stand, including experts who questioned the prosecution's physical evidence.

But Wayne Williams didn't have money to hire a dream team.

Wayne Williams was defended by court-appointed attorneys for the most part, who had little experience in murder cases.

Heading the defense team was criminal defense attorney Mary Welcome. Welcome was a popular local attorney and a former city solicitor, so she had trial experience and connections in the local legal community, but it was her first murder trial and from the beginning it was obvious that she was outmatched and over her head during the proceedings.

Welcome chose attorney Tony Axam to assist her because he had more experience trying major crimes. Although Axam was not considered a "high-powered" attorney by any stretch, he gave Williams' underfunded defense team some experience and legitimacy.

But for reasons that remain unclear, Williams decided to fire Axam before the trial.

Perhaps it was Williams' narcissistic personality getting the better of him, or maybe he thought that Alvin Binder, who replaced Axam, would do a better job, but it became crystal clear that Wayne Williams' defense team was in serious trouble even before the trial started.

Binder was an experienced trial lawyer from Mississippi who was known for his sometimes caustic and confrontational style. Throughout the course of Williams' trial, he was aggressive in his cross-examinations of witnesses, sometimes to the point where it created a cloud of tension in the courtroom.

The defense had to develop a strategy to overcome the mountain of physical and circumstantial evidence against their client. They didn't call any expert witnesses to refute the fiber evidence presented by the prosecution or offer any alternative interpretations, but they instead focused on the fact that none of it was 100% certain.

The defense also planned to call into question the credibility of the eyewitnesses.

Essentially, the defense was that Wayne Williams didn't commit any murders and that he was at the wrong place at the wrong time and was the victim of misidentification.

The defense put few experts on the stand who could refute the prosecution's experts. Although the defense did call some individuals who testified to Williams' alibis, they were few in number.

The defense was going to make the prosecution prove their case.

Because they planned to put very few witnesses on the stand and present very little evidence, the defense's case may have only lasted for a couple of days, but Wayne Williams made the major decision to take the stand in his own defense.

Williams' decision to take the stand extended the defense's case by three days.

When any type of criminal case goes to trial, most defense attorneys strongly advise their clients against taking the stand in their own defense. Although it is a constitutional right to take the stand, and there is a pervasive attitude that an innocent person would want to "sing it to the mountain" if accused of a crime, taking the stand opens one up to many problems.

Prosecutors are trained professionals who will verbally and intellectually destroy a defendant who is not ready for a grueling cross-examination. Also, everyone reacts differently in extreme situations. For instance, if a defendant doesn't show enough emotion, then he or she may be viewed as disconnected and therefore guilty. On the other hand, if a defendant shows too much emotion, it may seem forced and lacking in sincerity, therefore making the defendant look guilty.

But there was no way that Wayne Williams would be kept off the stand.

In Wayne Williams' mind, he was smarter than the prosecutors and all he had to do was answer a few simple questions to prove that he wasn't the Atlanta Child killer.

Williams probably didn't intend to be on the stand as long as he was.

The first two days he was on the stand, Williams kept his composure and came off as almost passive and timid. Williams was polite and quiet, even to the point where some of his answers were inaudible and needed to be repeated for the court reporter.

Many started to wonder if he could really be the one who killed so many people.

But things took a drastic change on his third day on the stand.

It was clear from an early point that Williams was becoming more frustrated and agitated on his third day. The prosecutors launched into him with more pointed questions, which changed Williams' demeanor from laid back to wound up and ready to pounce. He sat forward in his seat and his face went from more of a neutral countenance to a scowl.

Finally, Wayne Williams couldn't take it anymore – the Atlanta Child killer had to be unleashed.

"Do you want the real Wayne Williams? You got him," Williams shouted at the prosecutor in one particularly testy exchange.

Williams then followed the outburst up by referring to the prosecutor as a "dropshot."

In the inner-city black American vernacular of the time, a "dropshot" was someone who wasn't worthy of much. Coincidentally, one witness testified that Williams also referred to some of the children murdered in the Atlanta Child Murders case as dropshots.

It was apparently a word Williams liked to use, but it was starting to make him look bad.

As the vigorous cross-examination of Williams continued by the prosecution, Wayne grew even more frustrated by the line of questioning. Every question seemed to anger Williams and his tone became more combative. He tried to contain himself, but struck out once again when asked about Robert Henry's testimony.

"I done told you I don't hold hands with no man no where," Williams snapped when asked about holding hands with Cater.

Williams' third day of testimony on the stand made him look bad and in the eyes of some of the jurors, it helped cement the fact that they thought he was guilty. Simply put, his testimony was an unmitigated disaster.

Years later, Wayne Williams claimed that his lawyers told him he was being too passive for the first two days on the stand and that he needed to appear as though he was fighting for his life.

"I need you to be forceful on the stand. . . When he says something challenge it," Williams later claimed his lawyers said.

Instead of helping his cause, Williams played right into the prosecution's trap on the stand.

But Jack Mallard admitted that how Williams' behaved on the stand was not a foregone conclusion. Williams was intelligent enough and usually quite poised, which could have resulted in a testimony that would've helped him.

"He was a wily character. Smart, articulate the first two days and he controlled himself," Mallard reminisced about the chance that Williams would be able to help himself by taking the stand. "The third day he went into a tantrum."

Williams later admitted regret about taking the stand, maintaining that although the prosecution may have made him look bad, he never admitted guilt. In fact, in a 2010 interview Williams seemed to disregard the validity of the prosecution's entire case based on the fact that no one ever actually saw him kill any of the victims.

"The bottom line is, nobody ever testified or even claimed that they saw me strike another person, choke another person, stab, beat or kill or hurt anybody, because I didn't," said Williams in a 2010 interview.

Once Williams was done testifying, there was little more the defense could do. About the best evidence they presented on Williams' behalf were his parents, who testified that he was with them the night Nathaniel Cater was abducted.

After about eight weeks of trial, the case went to the jury.

The Verdict

The jury had a mountain of evidence to sift through, but of course most of it pointed toward Wayne Williams' guilt. On February 27, 1982, after only eleven hours of deliberation, the verdict was announced – guilty on both counts of first-degree murder.

No one really appeared very surprised.

The prosecutors looked relieved and several of the victims' family members in attendance at the trial also looked like a weight had been lifted off their backs, but the verdict was what most people expected.

Mary Welcome later claimed she "was crestfallen" when the verdict was announced, but that may be more of a professional lawyer talking than anything. Williams himself didn't look surprised as the verdict was read and he was taken back to the jail.

Wayne's father, William, did have a few things to say before he disappeared into obscurity. As he walked by the prosecution's table, he clearly called them "sons of bitches."

The insult didn't seem to faze Mallard or his team.

Wayne Williams was later given two life sentences to be served in the Georgia Department of Corrections.

The people of the city of Atlanta were finally able to breathe a sigh of relief, but if they thought they had heard the last of Wayne Williams or the Atlanta Child Murders case they were mistaken.

The Atlanta Child Murders case is truly a case that will not die.

CHAPTER 8:
Unresolved Issues

In most cases involving notable serial killers, the story for the most part ends once the killer is sent to prison. Sure, there are cases like Jeffrey Dahmer's, where his ultimate demise behind bars provided a final, interesting chapter in the saga, or at least a postscript. However, in most cases the killer is rarely heard from again and there are no major developments in the case.

Not so in the Atlanta Child Murders case.

Once Wayne Williams was sent to prison to serve his life sentence, it merely started another chapter in the story and it looks like there still may be at least one more to be written.

Many variables made the Atlanta Child Murders case different than previous and later serial killer cases in this respect.

The fact that there were numerous conspiracy theories circulating, even in the midst of Wayne Williams' killing spree, meant that not all would die a quick death, or even die at all, once Williams was convicted of Cater's and Payne's murders. Not long after Wayne Williams was sent away, some new twists on older theories began to circulate, partially helped by Williams himself.

And besides the often outlandish conspiracy theories, credible doubt remained that Williams was responsible for all twenty-eight murders.

The members of the Task Force, and the jury who decided Williams' fate, were unanimous that he killed Cater and Payne. Most members of the Task Force were also confident that Williams killed most of the other twenty-six victims. The combination of the physical evidence and the eyewitnesses accounts were just too much to ignore. Besides the two murders he was convicted of, most Task Force members were confident that he killed the ten "pattern" victims as well.

Although few members of the Task Force have stated publicly that they believe he killed all of them.

Determining if other killers may have been involved has unfortunately been clouded by a combination of egos, emotions, and sometimes racially charged political motives.

All of these issues, and more, have contributed to making the Atlanta Child Murders case the first major serial killer case that was tailor-made for American television.

A Public Cause

Today, celebrities get involved in so many causes it is difficult to keep up with them. Articulate, yet sanctimonious and self-righteous actors and musicians routinely grace us with their opinions on social media and lecture us while they receive awards for their artistic achievement. For the most part, these celebrities seem to talk so much about their opinions that they are ignored by most of the public. Most people are only interested in seeing and hearing these people perform, not listening to their opinions on geo-politics and other matters.

This is actually a fairly recent phenomenon.

Sure, actors and musicians became more politically opinionated and active during the 1960s, but they rarely preached their ideas to the masses and almost never mixed their craft with their opinions. In some ways the Atlanta Child Murders case was when that began to change. As discussed earlier, Frank Sinatra and Sammy Davis Junior performed a benefit on behalf of the victims' families and Muhammad Ali, Burt Reynolds, and Gladys Knight donated money to catch the killer.

Unlike some of the causes that celebrities support today, standing up for the victims of the Atlanta Child killer was apolitical and a cause that people from across the country would support if likable artists led the way.

After the success of Sinatra's and Davis Junior's concert, other celebrities decided to join the cause, eventually making it a true *cause celeb*.

Robert De Niro is known today just as much for his often outspoken, although not always insightful, political opinions on a host of issues as he is for his acting. In 1981, when he was nominated for an Oscar for best leading actor for his role in the film *Raging Bull*, he decided to take up the cause of Atlanta's murdered children. While Wayne Williams was still in the midst of his murder spree, De Niro won and accepted his award wearing a noticeable green ribbon on his jacket. When he was later asked by reporters about the ribbon's significance, he responded that it was to support the victims of the Atlanta Child Murders and their families.

It is one of the first known instances of celebrities wearing a ribbon for a specific cause.

Another notable example of public support for the victims and their families was a benefit concert given by the Jackson Five in Atlanta. Although the group had scheduled the concert months in advance, it just so happened that the night they performed—June 22—just so happened to be one day after the arrest of Wayne Williams. The mood in the concert was notably more upbeat than it would have been if Williams was on the loose, but it was still covered by a shroud of unease.

Williams did such an immense amount of damage to the psyche of the city of Atlanta that it would take decades to recover.

For years, Atlanta was known as the city "where all the kids were killed." The case definitely had a negative impact on the economy, as visitors and tourists avoided the Big Peach. Some say that the city only recovered its image when it hosted the 1996 Summer Olympic Games.

The case also negatively affected the long-term residents of Atlanta.

Although a minority, large segments of the population continued to believe that Williams was either set-up to take the fall for some larger, darker conspiracy and that the killer or killers were still on the loose. On the other side, most residents believed that Williams was the killer, but those with opposing opinions often clashed.

The difference in opinion concerning Williams' guilt was usually based along racial lines: most of those who believe a larger conspiracy was at work were black, while the overwhelming number of whites believed that Williams was a legitimate serial killer.

Williams' convictions went into the Georgia appellate court, eventually ending up in the Georgia Supreme Court where the case was decided in late 1983

New Hope for Wayne Williams

As Williams sat in prison, he developed a small but loyal following on the outside. Sure, there were several serial killer groupies who wrote him letters, but others supported him because they either believed, or wanted to believe he was innocent.

Wayne's parents would make the drive to visit their son in prison nearly every week until old age and health prevented them from doing so. A number of people who had never met Williams also supported him for various reasons. Some actually believed that he was set up in some type of elaborate, racist conspiracy that extended to the White House. Most of these people had their own agendas to pursue and were only using Williams as a vehicle for their cause.

However, there has been few people who have legitimately supported Williams over the years.

When Williams appealed his conviction, a small group of young, hungry lawyers got together to see what type of grounds they could argue for a new trial and they all agree that the trial judge allowing the prosecution to use the "pattern murders" as evidence was problematic.

Since Wayne Williams had not been convicted, or even charged with the crimes, the prosecution shouldn't have been allowed to use the cases or any physical evidence associated with them as evidence against Williams. The argument was rejected in the state appellate court, but then went to the Georgia Supreme Court where it was given a hearing.

Originally, there were two dissenting judges—Justice Richard Bell and Justice George Smith. Bell was assigned to draft the opinion in the case and although a former prosecutor, he wrote that Williams did not get a fair trial. The draft was rewritten and Bell changed his vote to uphold the conviction. Some sources say Bell was "pressured" to do so by the other judges, while other sources say he simply changed his opinion based on the facts.

Among Bell's criticisms of the original trial was the judge's allowing the use of the "pattern" murders. Bell was later quoted in 1985 by the *Washington Post* as saying:

"There was no evidence placing Williams with those five victims before their murders, and as in all the murders linked to Williams, there were no eyewitnesses, no confession, no murder weapons and no established motive. Also, the five deaths, while somewhat similar to each other in technique, were unlike the two for which Williams was tried."

Still, Bell voted to uphold, which left only one justice who dissented.

The dissenting judge, Justice Smith, later said in interviews that he believed the evidence from the "pattern murders" shouldn't have been allowed and that alone should've been enough for a new trial.

Smith said that allowing the other murders to be used as evidence "illustrates the basic unfairness of this trial and Williams' unenviable position as a defendant who, charged with two murders, was forced to defend himself as to twelve separate killing."

He also added that he didn't think the fiber evidence represented certainty.

Williams' attorneys argued valiantly for their client, but in the end the court was unimpressed and ruled six to one to uphold the conviction in December 1983.

The appeal represented Williams best hope for a new trial.

A Red Herring

As soon as Wayne Williams was assigned a cell block in the Hancock State Prison in Sparta, Georgia, he went to work on his appeals. It wasn't like Williams had much to work with – the combined corpus of evidence against him was overwhelming – but the clever killer had a few tricks up his sleeve.

He could attack the trial judge for permitting the use of evidence in other murders for which he wasn't convicted or even charged – the so-called "pattern murders."

Williams could also dredge up some of the old conspiracy theories.

When one is as desperate as Wayne Williams, conspiracy theories can be utilized and exploited to one's own ends.

For Williams, the Klan conspiracy was perfect.

Although the Task Force investigated the Klan angle in 1981, and another victim was actually killed while they were doing their surveillance, it is a theory that just won't go away for a number of reasons. First, although in 1981 the Klan was but a shadow of its size during its peak in the 1920s, it had continued to serve as the consummate boogeyman in American culture. Images of toothless, violent Klansmen are common in the American media, which is of course bolstered by numerous real acts of violence committed by the organization since the 1860s. Second, many of the black residents refused to believe that a black serial killer could exist and to them there was certainly no way a mild-mannered, articulate young man like Wayne Williams could be the killer.

For many, it was a matter of perception and long-held beliefs.

Quite simply, the Klan theory wasn't going away.

The original Klan theory and investigation was focused on a man named Charles T. Sanders. In many ways, Sanders would've been the perfect foil for the Atlanta Child murders as he fit the stereotypical profile of a Klansmen in many ways. He was a lifelong, avowed militant racist and came from a family with heavy connections in the criminal underworld.

Sanders and his brothers, who were also Klansmen, had compiled impressive criminal records by 1981 that included arrests and convictions for assault, weapons violations, drugs, and sex crimes. When Sanders wasn't running the Klan, he was running drugs and/or guns, or drinking heavily and running his mouth in a number of bars just outside Atlanta.

However, Sanders was far from a criminal mastermind.

The "Klan" that he ran was little more than a dozen guys, about half of whom were either informants or actual agents with several different law enforcement agencies. Although Sanders' group had ties to other organizations throughout the southeast, the Klan of the late 1970s and early 1980s was but a shadow of its former self. Even to other white supremacists the Klan seemed old fashioned and out of touch with the times.

Sanders and his brothers seemed more interested in moving drugs and guns than doing any "traditional" Klan activity, which is actually how they came to the attention of law enforcement.

The fact that Sanders' Klan was so heavily infiltrated by law enforcement is what put him on the Task Force's radar in the first place. One of the many informants in the Klan put in a call to his handler one day that sounded interesting. The informant was a career criminal named Billy Joe Whitaker. Whitaker may have been racist, but his involvement with Sanders and the Klan was the result of drugs and other criminal activity. Throughout his long career as a criminal, Whitaker learned that it was easier to cooperate with the police in order to reduce his sentence.

He would also get paid from time to time.

Although Whitaker wasn't an official member of Sander's Klan group, he claimed to the Task Force that he was a confident and privy to personal and secret conversation.

According to Whitaker, Sanders praised the murders of the black children, saying that the killer has erased "generations of niggers." Whitaker also claimed that Sanders knew victim Lubie Geter as they were neighbors. He also claimed that Sanders had a grudge against the child because Geter supposedly ran into Sander's car with a go-kart.

The comments were certainly offensive and the connection to Geter was interesting, but Sanders was after all a Klan member and his speech is protected by the First Amendment. And although Sander's connection to Geter was interesting, it wasn't evidence of anything.

Most of the Task Force didn't think there was much to the Klan angle, but after some pressure they diverted several of their resources and began doing around the clock surveillance of the group.

The surveillance teams followed Sanders and the other Klansmen to meetings where they discussed a number of things, but never the Atlanta Child Murders. The Task Force observed Sanders and others commit several weapons violations, but never murder or even an assault.

"These family members were under surveillance at that time, physical surveillance, where we had an eyeball on them," said Bob Ingraham who led the GBI stakeout of the group.

The Task Force eventually decided to show their hand by bringing Sanders, his brothers, and some of the members of their group in for questioning. Although the Klansmen were under no obligation to talk to the Task Force, they all willingly complied and agreed to take polygraph exams.

They all passed.

With no evidence linking Sanders and his Klan buddies to any of the murders, the Task Force decided to move on and focus on other leads. While they were investigating the Klan angle six more black boys were murdered, one while almost all of their resources were devoted to a stakeout of Sanders.

For the most part, the Klan angle was forgotten when Williams was sent away to prison. No one involved in the case gave the theory any serious thought, including Williams defense attorneys who never even bothered to raise the issue as part of his defense.

But the angle was just too salacious to go away and it was a perfect story to sell some magazines.

In 1986, *Spin* magazine published a feature article titled "A Question of Justice" by Robert Keating and Barry Michael Cooper that brought the Klan conspiracy theory back into the forefront and helped to reopen the Wayne Williams' case.

The thesis of the article was that although Wayne Williams may have committed the murders he was convicted of, Charles Sanders and his local Klan group were responsible for up to fifteen of the child murders. They wrote that the murders were part of an elaborate plot by Sanders and his cohorts to incite a race war in Atlanta that would spread across the country. The Klansmen would begin by killing one black boy a month, while stockpiling weapons for the wider civil conflict.

Using questionable sources and innuendos, the reporters based their whole theory on the fact that Charles Sanders *may* have threatened Lubie Geter. The article for the most part didn't address obvious problems with the theory, such as the most glaring one—how could Klan hit crews move in and out of all black neighborhoods without being noticed?

The article further claimed that the Klan conspiracy was covered up because the city leaders didn't want Atlanta to descend into racial violence. Never mind that the city leaders were almost all black.

Finally, on the one hand the article portrayed Sanders and his Klan as low IQ rubes and losers in life, but on the other hand as having enough agency to develop an elaborate plot to start a race war. The practicality of the race war "plot" were also never considered by the writers. How would killing one black boy a month start a race war if no one ever took credit for the murders?

Although the Klan theory was nothing new, the *Spin* article brought the theory to a wider audience, which ultimately helped Williams get his case back into court in 1991. Notable leftist attorney, the late William Kunstler took Williams' case *pro bono*, along with Alan Dershowitz, who is better known for being one of the members of O.J. Simpson's "Dream Team."

Since most of what was written in the *Spin* article was a combination of hearsay, embellishments, and outright lies, little of it could be used by Williams' lawyers. The primary piece of evidence they used as an argument for their client to get a new trial were statements by the drug addict Klan informant. The informant told Williams' lawyers that he once overheard Sanders brag about strangling a black youth to death who was not classified as one of the Atlanta Child Murders victims.

Due to the informant's questionable background and the fact that he had changed his story more than once, Williams was denied a new trial.

Although the Klan conspiracy theory had its last mention in the courts by the late 1980s, Williams still claims that he was set up as part of a racist conspiracy.

"Atlanta, at the time, was in a panic. They wanted any suspect that they could find and let's just be honest, it had to be a black person because if it had been a white suspect Atlanta probably would have gone up in flames, it came very close to that." said Williams in a 2010 interview.

The denial of a new trial based on the Klan theory didn't stop Wayne Williams from continuing his legal fight and it didn't put to rest the theory in many people's minds.

Other Possible Killers

Few familiar with the Atlanta Child Murders case believe that Wayne Williams is an innocent man. There is little doubt that Williams is a murderer and he very likely killed enough children to earn the title of the Atlanta Child Killer, but is he responsible for all twenty-eight of the murders?

Even if the Klan is not considered a viable suspect in some of the murders, the likelihood that one or more of the murders attributed to the series were actually committed by someone other than Wayne Williams is not so small.

Atlanta is and was then a dangerous city with a high crime rate, with most of the crime taking place in black neighborhoods.

An examination of the murder cases individually reveals that some didn't fit Wayne Williams' M.O. and a review of statements made by members of the Task Force shows that opinion varied on how many people were involved.

As was already discussed earlier, on the eve of the arrest of Wayne Williams, the Atlanta Police Department publicly stated that it believed Williams was assisted in his murders. This view was shared to an extent by others on the Task Force.

Robbie Hamrick, the former director of the Georgia Bureau of Investigation, who worked on the Task Force, had little doubt that Wayne Williams murdered Nathaniel Cater and Jimmy Ray Payne, but he is not so sure about how many of the other twenty-eight victims were his.

"I'm convinced he was responsible for the two cases he was convicted on," Hamrick said. "The others -- that's something the courts would have to decide."

Chet Dettlinger also doubted if Williams was responsible for killing all of the victims. Like Hamrick and some other skeptics on the Task Force, Dettlinger believed that Williams was a murderer, and most likely a serial killer, but that not all of the murders could be attributed to him.

Despite the doubts among some on the Task Force, the still living prosecutors who worked the case believe that Wayne Williams was the Atlanta Child Killer. In a 2010 interview, Jack Mallard explained that the reason why they only prosecuted Williams for the murders of Cater and Payne was because those were the most solid cases they had. He further added that he was confident Williams was responsible for most, if not all, of the twenty-eight murders and that if he were given a proper amount of time to prepare, he could have secured convictions on Williams for fifteen to twenty of the murders.

Still, some of the details in a few of the cases didn't add up and there was a case or two that just didn't seem to fit.

The case that stood out the most as not having fit with the rest of the Atlanta Child Murders was the murder of seven-year-old Latonya Wilson. Latonya was abducted from the bedroom of her apartment on June 22, 1980, during the height of the murders. Her skeletal remains were discovered over a month later in a vacant lot, leading the investigators to conclude that she was another victim of the Atlanta Child Murders.

The discovery of Latonya's body in a vacant lot was about the only thing her murder had in common with the other Atlanta Child Murders cases. But since she was a child and her body was discovered in a vacant lot, Latonya was added to the list.

The fact that Latonya was a girl was a red flag to most skeptics that her murder was not part of the series. Although another girl, Angel Lenair, is also listed as a victim of the Atlanta Child murderer, the fact that there are only two seems to be the classic case of the exception proving the rule.

If Wayne Williams was a repressed homosexual serial killer who took his sexual and racial frustrations out on black boys and young black men as the profilers said, why did he deviate from his dark crusade by killing Wilson and Lenair?

More importantly, the killer's M.O. in the Wilson case didn't match any of the twenty-eight murders on the list.

The standard M.O. in the Atlanta Child Murders case was that Williams would seduce a boy or young man with some type of business, money, or possibly sexual offer to get him into his car. He would then murder his quarry, disrobe the body, and then dump the body in a river or wooded lot.

In the Wilson case, the abductor boldly broke into the victim's family's apartment through her bedroom window. The abductor then took Wilson from the apartment to the complex's parking lot, where a witness claimed to have seen him talking to another man.

Besides the case having a totally different victimology and M.O., the abductor(s) of Latoya Wilson appear to have had intimate knowledge of not just the apartment complex where the Wilson family lived, but also Wilson's apartment.

It could very well be that Latoya Wilson abductor(s) and killer(s) were people she knew.

Certain details of the murder of Eric Middlebrooks also don't fit Wayne Williams' standard M.O., which is important because the first carpet fiber was found on the bottom of his shoe.

Although Middlebrooks certainly fit the victimology of the Atlanta

Child Murders case, the manner in which he was killed and where and how his body was discovered did not.

Middlebrooks' body was discovered the day after he disappeared, not in a river or a vacant lot, but behind the offices of a Georgia Department of Corrections parole center. The nature of the building itself would be enough to draw suspicions in most other cases, but instead the murder was quickly assigned to the Atlanta Child Murders case.

Also, unlike the vast majority of Williams' victims, who were suffocated or strangled, Middlebrooks was beaten to death. His pockets were also turned inside out as if he were robbed or someone was trying to find something they believed he was carrying.

The only aspects of the Middlebrooks murder that seemed to match any of the other cases was that he was murdered at another location and then dumped where he was discovered. The fiber found on his shoe also matched fibers on other victims and those from rugs and carpets in the Williams home.

For those reasons, the murder of Eric Middlebrooks was assigned to Wayne Williams.

Another one of the cases that many in the community doubted at the time was the murder of thirteen-year-old Clifford Jones. Clifford disappeared on August 20, 1980 and his strangled body was discovered at a later date in a wooded lot.

Most of the aspects of the Jones case fit the victimology and M.O. of Wayne Williams, but witnesses were adamant that they saw Jones leave with a white man, who was later determined to be a convicted sex offender. The Task Force followed the lead up, but later stated that the man in question was actually misidentified and that they were confident Wayne Williams killed Clifford Jones.

Not everyone in Atlanta was convinced, though.

Accomplices?

The idea that Wayne Williams was not responsible for all twenty-eight of the murders on the list is very probable when one even gives a cursory examination of some of the more questionable cases. Even Jack Mallard admitted that he would only a secure a conviction on at most twenty of the murders.

This then raises another question – could Wayne Williams have been working with others?

At first glance, the question doesn't really seem to fit Wayne Williams' personality. He was a consummate loner who was not known to have any romantic partners and very few friends. Williams would seem like the last person who would work with others, but when it comes to murder anything is possible.

There are numerous examples of serial killers working in pairs, such as the "Speed Freak Killers," Loren Herzog and Wesley Shermantine, in California during the 1980s and 1990s, or even in groups, like the "Ripper Crew" of early 1980s Chicago. Some of these pair and group serial killers were for the most part loners, but they put aside their misanthropy to commit organized murder.

Serial killers working in pairs and groups are much more common than one may think.

It is estimated that up to twenty-five percent of all serial murders are committed by a pair or group. The numbers indicate that there is a *possibility* that some of the twenty-eight murders attributed to the Atlanta Child Murders case could have been committed by a serial killer pair or group.

There have been persistent rumors that Wayne Williams worked with an accomplice to kill at least two of his victims.

When Jeffrey Mathis disappeared off the face of the earth on the evening of March 11, 1980, there was a witness who saw him get into a car. The description of the car closely matched Wayne Williams' white station wagon and the description of the driver matched Williams, but the witness also described a darker skinned black male in the car with Williams.

A similar description was given by a witness when Aaron Wyche disappeared on the night of June 23, 1980. In that case, the witness described Wyche get into a white station wagon with two young adult black males.

The Task Force attributed both murders to Williams, but added that there is no evidence he had assistance. The Task Force rightfully pointed out that witness identification is often complicated by several factors, such as the young age of the witnesses in these cases.

The Task Force believes that the witnesses were simply confused.

Other Conspiracies?

Besides the debunked Klan conspiracy theory, numerous other theories cropped up during and after the killings that propose numerous other groups of people were involved in some of the murders. Since Atlanta is a high-crime city and plenty of its residents have criminal records, there was no shortage of people who were accused of playing a role in the Atlanta Child Murders.

Some of the more sensationalistic of the theories held that members of Atlanta's black elite were murdering the children as part of an organized pedophile ring.

The more believable theories pointed to numerous Atlanta ex-convicts with records of sex offenses and pedophilia.

One of the first non-Klan conspiracy theories involving the Atlanta Child Murders developed during Wayne Williams trial. The conspiracy theory began when a Miami woman called the Task Force claiming that her former boyfriend admitted to the murders of twenty-one-year-old Eddie Duncan and twenty-one-year-old Larry Rogers.

The call was immediately given credence because it was made before the bodies of the men were discovered.

The story that the woman told to the Task Force investigators made her seem less credible, though, in their eyes because it sounded like something out one of the *Purge* movies. The woman claimed that her boyfriend, who was black, was paid handsomely by unknown people to abduct black boys and young black men and then to deliver them live to a group of white people, who would ostensibly murder the victims.

The woman's boyfriend also claimed to have dumped some of the bodies once the mysterious murderous white people had their fun.

The theory sounded outlandish to nearly every agent on the Task Force. Although the woman made the call before the bodies of the men were discovered, their disappearances were publicized so the investigators wrote the entire thing off as another case of someone trying to seek attention.

But there were still other conspiracy theories the investigators had to consider.

One of the more elaborate conspiracy theories investigated by the Task Force involved a potential organized pedophile ring led by members of Atlanta's black elite. According to the theory, several members of the black business community, as well as some government officials, were paying young men with criminal records to abduct black children on the streets of Atlanta. The children were then brought to members of the ring where they were abused and murdered before being given back to the abductors, who then dumped the bodies in wooded areas and rivers around the Atlanta metro area.

There was little evidence of the theory other than some vague rumors on the streets, but the case took a temporarily interesting turn when the body of twenty-three-year-old Michael McIntosh was discovered in an Atlanta area river in late March 1981.

Despite his age, McIntosh was added to the list of other victims in the Atlanta Child Murders case because his murder fit the M.O. of the killer. Although an adult, McIntosh was still relatively young and not very big physically. His body was discovered nude and the coroner later determined that he had been strangled to death like most of the other victims.

A search into McIntosh's background led to the investigation of the organized black elite pedophilia theory.

McIntosh had already compiled a considerable criminal record in his young life. Although most of the crimes he committed were property related, he lived on the edges of society and knew some pretty shady characters in the criminal underground. Like most of the other adult victims in the series, McIntosh was a drug user and heavy drinker who was known to resort to prostitution for his next fix.

One of those associates had some pretty interesting things to say to the police.

The informant told the Task Force that McIntosh may have been murdered by some people who hired him. The person then went on to describe the organized black elite pedophile ring and how it worked.

According to the informant, McIntosh was one of the young men who was paid to abduct and deliver young boys to the group and then later dump their bodies. McIntosh was apparently killed because he knew too much.

The Task Force worked the organized pedophile angle for a while, with many of the investigators believing it, but it was eventually dropped. They could find no evidence that tied the petty criminal McIntosh to any members of Atlanta's elite black society. Other than the questionable informant, the Task Force found no evidence at all of an organized pedophilia ring that was responsible for any of the deaths in the Atlanta Child Murders case.

Like the Klan theory, the organized pedophilia theory appeared to be another red herring.

Another angle that the Task Force had to investigate, which looked promising at the time, involved a career criminal named Larry Marshal.

In 1981, Larry Marshal was thirty-four and well acquainted with the criminal justice system as he had racked up a series of arrests and convictions for crimes ranging from drugs to aggravated assault and from property crimes to sex crimes.

Larry Marshal was not a nice man.

After Marshal's name came up in the investigation, investigators were able to prove that he knew three of the Atlanta Child Murders victims: Patrick Baltazar, Jojo Bell, and thirteen-year-old Timothy Hill.

Hill lived in the same neighborhood as Baltazar and Bell and was often seen with the other two boys, playing basketball and working hustles at the local grocery store and seafood restaurant. Like the other two boys, Hill had little adult supervision and was known to run the streets all hours of the night until he disappeared on March 13, 1981.

Hill's partially decomposed nude body was later discovered in a river. The coroner ruled that he had been suffocated, so the Task Force added him to the list.

When the investigators learned that Larry Marshal knew Baltazar, Bell, and Hill, they dug deeper to learn the nature of the relationships.

What they discovered was truly disturbing.

Besides selling drugs, robbing stores and people, and breaking into homes, Larry Marshal was a pimp. He ran a brothel in southwest Atlanta that catered to men with varied "tastes." He employed both males and females in his bordello and was even known to offer the services of underage boys.

Patrick Baltazar, Jojo Bell, and Timothy Hill were all said to have worked in the brothel at different times.

Marshal was easy to track down in 1981 because he was facing a plethora of felony charges in more than one jurisdiction. In the spring of 1981 Marshal was in a Hartford, Connecticut jail facing felony charges and was wanted for an armed robbery and stabbing in Atlanta unrelated to the Atlanta Child Murders case.

Members of the Task Force traveled to Connecticut to interview Marshal and quickly determined that he could not have personally killed any of the three boys.

Opportunists?

When the other Atlanta Child Murders theories are ruled out as too outlandish and lacking in any evidence, it becomes clear that Wayne Williams was good for fifteen to twenty of the killings as Jack Mallard said.

However, that still leaves open the possibility that up to a dozen of the murders were committed by someone, or some people, other than Wayne Williams.

Even people who believe Wayne Williams is the Atlanta Child Killer think that around half dozen of the murders on the list may have been isolated. It is difficult to contemplate, but the reality is that a few of the murders may have been committed by coldblooded opportunists.

The sad reality is that the overwhelming percentage of child murder victims are killed by someone close to them, usually a parent. Atlanta was no different than most places in the United

States in that respect and as Mike Edward, the Deputy Director of the Atlanta Criminal Investigations Division at the time noted, most of those cases were closed.

"In Atlanta, if I remember my stats right . . . up until that we had generally seen, I'd want to say six or nine kids killed a year by relatives," said Edward. "And we had about a 90% conviction rate, maybe ninety-five."

Edward is one of the Task Force members who believed that at least a few domestic murders were added to the official list of Atlanta Child Murders victims. He pointed out that although the overwhelming number of victims' bodies were found in an around wooded areas during the first year and a half of the spree, some of the lots were located close to homes.

In other words, it would have been convenient for a parent or family member to kill a child in a fit of rage, or even premeditated, and then dump the body in a nearby vacant lot to make it look like another victim of the Atlanta Child Killer.

None of these alternate ideas and theories prove Wayne Williams is innocent – they only show that there is little likelihood that there was another serial killer, or killers, operating in Atlanta at the time. What these theories do show, though, is that Williams probably didn't commit all twenty-eight of the murders and that at least a couple of people got away with murder.

Wayne Williams continues to plead his innocence from behind prison walls.

CHAPTER 9:
New Revelations

After Williams' request for a new trial based on the Klan theory was denied and the Georgia Supreme Court denied him a new trial due to the "pattern murders" evidence, Wayne Williams and the Atlanta Child Murders case receded from the consciousness of most Americans for the 1990s.

Williams continued to tell his stories to whoever would listen, but by the early 2000s few were interested. There was no compelling new evidence that pointed toward his innocence or even the existence of other conspirators.

There were also no more salacious stories to report associated with the case.

Since newspapers, which were still the primary media in the 1990s, papers sell by reporting interesting stories, there was no reason to report anything about the case because nothing new or interesting was happening.

To most people during the 1990s and early 2000s, Wayne Williams and the Atlanta Child Murders "were so 1980s."

It was time to move on.

But then the case was given new life in 2005.

A New Investigation

On May 6, 2005, Dekalb County Police Chief Louis Graham announced that his office was reopening the investigation into some of the murders in the Atlanta Child Murders case. Dekalb County borders Fulton County/Atlanta, just to the west where a few of the victims were from and where some of the bodies were discovered. Although all of those murders were officially closed and attributed to Wayne Williams, there was pressure from some quarters of the community to reopen them.

And the office of county police chief is extremely political.

Almost from the beginning, Chief Graham faced many accusations concerning his reasons for reopening the cases.

To begin with, Graham was not particularly good at his job – the crime rate in the county went up on his watch and there were several accusations of police misconduct. There were also rumors that Graham made borderline unethical decisions on the job. Because of these accusations, some in the Atlanta area thought that Graham only reopened the case to divert attention from his own problems.

For his part, Graham denied any personal reasons for reopening the cases, stating he honestly believed Wayne Williams may be innocent.

Along with the accusations of deflection, others argued that

Graham only opened the case for purely political reasons.

Some Atlantans argued that Graham, who is black, was blinded by his own prejudice and was also pressured by a vocal minority in the Atlanta black community who wanted to dredge up the Klan theory. Although most of the family members of the Atlanta Child Murders victims believed Wayne Williams was the killer, and the majority of the black community gave up on the Klan conspiracy theory once all the facts were revealed, a significant minority held onto the theory.

Graham publicly announced that the Klan theory was once again being investigated.

The police chief was a bit disingenuous, though, as he suggested that key witnesses had not been interviewed and potentially important evidence had not been considered by the Task Force in 1981. Graham was further aided by the Internet, as numerous websites that claimed the validity of the Klan theory began appearing.

Still, it's impossible to make a case where there isn't one.

The investigation didn't turn up any new evidence and there was little chance anything could've come from it anyway. Sanders' ex-wife claimed that he and most of his family members were dead by 2005. The revelation was not a surprise, but definitely a roadblock for pursuing the Klan angle.

Graham's investigation went nowhere and was closed on July 21, 2006.

The police chief then resigned and was replaced by Nick Marinelli.

The rumor was that Graham was asked to resign, partly due to his persistence to use the department's resources pursuing the Klan theory when there was no justification to do so.

After taking over as police chief, Marinelli gave a statement about the new investigation.

"We dredged up what we had and nothing has panned out, so until it does or additional evidence comes our way, or there's forensic feedback from existing evidence, we will continue to pursue the [other] cold cases that are [with]in our reach."

That was the last time Marinelli mentioned the investigation.

Not long after Graham announced a new investigation of the cases in Dekalb County, Wayne Williams filed a writ of *habeas corpus*. A writ of *habeas corpus* is simply a legal process by which an imprisoned person can request a hearing whereby the state must explain why that person is imprisoned. In Wayne Williams' case, it was essentially a last-ditch appeal. Since Williams had exhausted all of his traditional appeals, he filed the writ as another appeal.

In his legal brief, Williams brought up several issues he had already raised in his previous appeals. He also added that he should be given a new trial based on some evidence that was withheld at trial. One of the primary arguments he made, though, was based on Louis Graham's new investigation in Dekalb County.

Williams argued that the fact that a law enforcement agency was giving a new look at some of the evidence meant that there was significant doubt about his guilt and that he therefore should be given a new trial.

United States District Court Judge Beverly Martin disagreed.

In her February 2006 ruling against Williams' request for a new hearing, she wrote that most of the issues raised by Williams, such as the Klan conspiracy theory, had already been considered either at trial or in other appeals and that there was no reason to consider them presently.

The withheld evidence was probably Williams' best chance for a new trial, but Judge Martin didn't find that convincing either. She wrote that none of the withheld evidence "would have had more than a minimal impact upon the outcome of Mr. Williams' trial had it been presented to the jury."

Wayne Williams had to go back to the drawing board.

Back to Normal

Lost in all the discussions about conspiracy theories, opportunist killers, and the real number of people Wayne Williams killed, is probably the most obvious question: did the killings stop after Williams was arrested?

The answer is somewhat complicated, but for the most part the answer is yes.

Black children continued to be murdered in Atlanta, but the perpetrators were nearly always caught, as was pointed out by

Mike Edward, and the killers were almost always family members or someone close to the victims.

The early 1980s saw the overall crime rate in the United States drop with longer, "get tough on crime" sentences handed down by judges beginning in the late 1970s, but juvenile crime actually rose and it was much worse in the black community. Gang violence also became much more organized and pronounced during the 1980s, which has claimed the lives of many of Atlanta's black children.

However, even with those considerations, there were not nearly as many children murdered annually in the city in the years following the Atlanta Child Murders and the sex of the victims was not overwhelmingly male.

Finally, the manner in which the children were killed and dumped came to a sudden end once Wayne Williams was taken off the streets.

"The murders stopped and there has been nothing since," said prosecutor Joseph Drolet referring to the manner in which Williams killed his victims.

Welcome Harris, a black detective with the Atlanta Police Department who was on the Task Force, was also later asked if the killings came to an end after Williams was arrested. Specifically, Harris was asked how many black boys were killed in a similar manner after Williams' arrest, answering "none that I recall."

Harris worked in the homicide department of the Atlanta Police for twenty-five years after the Atlanta Child Murders case.

Lewis Slaton, who was a Fulton County attorney on the team that prosecuted Williams also noted that no fibers similar to those found in Wayne Williams' house and car were found on any of the murdered children in later years, which he believes "was a powerful argument to me" that they had the right man.

From his prison cell, Wayne Williams of course claims that the murders continued and the "list" should've been much longer.

"There are about forty-two cases, that had I not been arrested, would have been part of this list."

Wayne Williams is always looking for a new angle and anyone who will listen to his stories and alternate theories.

Wayne Williams in Prison

As soon as Williams was sentenced, he was loaded onto a prison bus and entered the Georgia Department of Corrections. Most inmates in any prison system in America are usually housed in several different prisons, depending on their custody classification, before they are released.

But for inmates serving life sentences, there is little movement.

The Valdosta State Prison, which is located near the Georgia-Florida state line outside Valdosta, Georgia, is where Williams began serving his life sentence. The prison is what is referred to as a "close security" prison, meaning that it is above the medium security but below maximum security. It has had its share of gang and racial violence over the years.

And Wayne Williams walked into the cauldron as a marked man.

Child molesters are at the bottom of the food chain in the inmate hierarchy in every American prison and child killers are barely a notch above them. Besides being marked as a well-known child killer, Williams had no known criminal underworld connections when he entered prison and was only 5'6 with a slight build.

Little is known about Williams' first few years in Valdosta State Prison and he has not been forthcoming about it in the few interviews he has given since being incarcerated, but the reality is that he now appears fine. There were rumors that emerged that he was physically and/or sexually assaulted when he first came to prison, but there are no signs of that being the case today. In fact, if anything, it appears that Williams has actually developed a certain amount of influence behind bars.

Wayne Williams may not be very big or tough, but he is smart enough to con some cons, which is what he has apparently done.

Four years after Williams was convicted, around the time the *Spin* article came out and he was making his first major legal push for a new trial, a key witness from the trial made a startling admission.

Robert Henry, the man who testified to having seen Nathaniel Cater and Wayne Williams holding hands the night Cater disappeared, gave Williams' attorneys a signed affidavit claiming that his original testimony was a lie. Williams also changed his alibi, stating that he was at a recording studio in a neighboring town the night Cater disappeared.

As discussed earlier, the appeal was rejected, with the appellate court stating that the Klan conspiracy theory was without merit and that any changes in witness testimony would not have affected the verdict.

Henry's changing story was largely forgotten until the late 2000s when interest in the Atlanta Child Murders was renewed following the thirty-year anniversary.

When Henry was asked by reporters why he changed his testimony, he somewhat evasively stated that he was intimated to do so by one of Wayne Williams' associates. It turns out that in 1986 Henry was also serving time in the Valdosta State Prison and although the prison authorities made sure to keep him in a separate cell block from Williams, the Atlanta Child Killer had apparently developed enough reach to intimidate Henry.

Henry further stated that he was given a pre-written statement and told to sign it.

"Those are words I was told to say," recalled Henry about the affidavit.

Clearly Wayne Williams had learned how to navigate his dangerous environment by 1986.

Perhaps due to his unwanted influence among the prison population, Williams was transferred to the Hancock State Prison in the 1990s, which is near the central Georgia town of Sparta.

Almost from the date it opened in 1991, Hancock State Prison rightfully earned a reputation as one of the toughest and most corrupt prisons in the southeast. Hancock has been the sight of numerous gang and racial conflicts, which were often the result of inmates fighting over contraband drugs, cell phones, or both.

Despite being a relatively new prison, authorities with the Georgia Department of Corrections have stated that up to twenty-eight percent of the locks on inmate cells don't work properly. Of course, the problems with the locks can lead to escape risks, but even more so it can create more inmate on inmate violence. Cell door locks are intended just as much to protect inmates from each other as they are to prevent escapes. The problems with the locks exposed inmate violence and contraband problems, which in turn exposed greater institutional problems.

The prison has also been a hotbed of official corruption.

Some guards have been implicated in schemes to smuggle drugs and cellphones into the prison for inmates and others have been accused of stoking the flames of violence among the inmates. All of the accusations of official misconduct at the prison led to a major investigation by the United States Department of Justice and eventually a 2016 FBI sting.

The FBI sting led to the arrests of several guards, whom the FBI alleges were smuggling phones and drugs into the prison for hefty fees from the inmate gang leaders. After the gang leaders got the drugs and phones, they would distribute them for princely fees to the other inmates.

Wayne Williams was using one of those phones in 2016.

Vincent Hill is a former private investigator who is now trying his hand at a new career as a true crime writer. The Atlanta Child Murders case always intrigued him, so he decided that it was as good a case as any to use for his first book. Since the only person convicted of any crimes associated with the case is still alive, Hill began his research by contacting Wayne Williams.

After writing letters to Williams and receiving noncommittal answers, he received a strange phone call one evening from a man claiming to be Wayne Williams. Since Hill was acquainted with justice system and prison life from his time as a PI, he knew that inmates can only make calls at certain times on special phones, where the person receiving the call is usually greeted with a pre-recorded prompt that states something to the effect, "Will you accept a call from an inmate in Valdosta State Prison?"

Hill talked to the man and quickly realized that it was in fact Wayne Williams to whom he was speaking. Williams explained to him that cell phones were fairly common in the prison and if one knew the right people then one could pay to use a phone.

It may hurt some of the families of the victims, but Wayne Williams has obviously learned how to survive and thrive in prison. However he did it, Williams successfully navigated the first few years of his sentence, which would've been the toughest, and is now a respected, yet infamous, man among his peers.

Although Williams has found time to use contraband cell phones and intimidate his fellow inmates, he spends most of his free time trying to win his release.

New DNA Testing

It is hard to say if Wayne Williams actually believes that he will be released from prison one day. In the few interviews he has given since his incarceration, he has been adamant that he *knows* he will be released one day. Of course, this is all part of the elaborate public facade that he has built over the years—he couldn't possibly admit any guilt at this point.

But he may actually believe it.

The reality is that if you tell yourself something enough times, even if it isn't true and you initially don't believe it, you will eventually begin to believe it. And when it comes to narcissists like Wayne Williams, it is often difficult to tell when they are telling the truth and when they are lying.

But DNA never lies.

When Williams was arrested and convicted of murder in the early 1980s, DNA profiling was not available to law enforcement. At that point, scientists knew that each person carried a unique deoxyribonucleic acid (DNA) code, but they had no way of reading it, so evidence that is today usually considered "DNA evidence" – hairs, blood, skin, etc. – could only be matched to type, if at all. All this changed when British scientist Alec Jeffreys discovered DNA profiling in 1984. By the late 1980s, DNA profiling was being used in criminal cases, although it would often take weeks or months to match a sample to a suspect and it was very expensive.

By the late 2000s, DNA profiling was available to all law enforcement agencies at a reasonable price and the process only took days, at the most, instead of months to complete.

Wayne Williams has had plenty of time to read about changes in the American criminal justice system, including the impact of DNA profiling.

DNA has set many wrongly convicted people free.

Could it set Wayne Williams free, or ensure that he stays behind bars for the rest of his life?

Wayne Williams talked a big game concerning DNA profiling of the evidence in his case during a 1999 interview.

"If you want to prove that Wayne Williams did this conclusively, let's get the DNA tests," said Williams in his usually defiant tone referring to himself in third person. "But if the DNA tests say this was not their blood, we need to go back to court."

The problem is that not all of the physical evidence used at Williams' trial has survived the test of time.

But two hairs were preserved well enough to be tested by accredited labs in the late 2000s.

A hair taken from the body of Patrick Baltazar was sent to a DNA testing lab and came back with somewhat mixed results. Although the hair could not be conclusively tied to Wayne Williams, it pointed toward him.

The test showed that less than three percent of the black American population had DNA that was consistent with hair.

Wayne Williams is in that three percent.

Some of the dog hairs found on Baltazar's body were also sent to an independent lab for DNA testing. Legally speaking, DNA profiling of animals is viewed similar to that of humans and has been used in numerous cases. The problem with the hairs taken from the Baltazar case was that they were degraded due to time so the test wouldn't be as precise.

Scientists at the University of California DNA lab were able to extract enough mitochondrial DNA from the dog hair to develop a general profile. The results showed that there was a ninety-nine percent chance that the hair came from the Williams family's German Shepard.

The combined DNA results certainly didn't bode well for Wayne Williams.

When asked about the results in later interviews, Williams brushed them off and instead focused on the fact that the human hair discovered on Patrick Baltazar couldn't be positively attributed to him.

Williams for the most part disregarded the dog hair evidence.

For many who were on the fence about Williams being the Atlanta Child Murders killer, it pushed them in the direction to see him as guilty. With that said, there are still many who cling to the conspiracy theories.

Conspiracy theories are more interesting, right?

The Atlanta Child Murders in Popular Media

As is the case with any high-profile murder case, the Atlanta Child Murders spawned several true crime books, many of which were written by people who worked on the case. Most of these books came to the conclusion that Wayne Williams was definitely guilty of the two murders for which he was convicted and probably guilty of most, if not all of the Atlanta Child Murders.

Not every true crime book about the case took that stance, though.

The renewed interest in the Atlanta Child Murders case in the late 1990s and early 2000s was largely the result of the internet. Several websites dedicated to the case have gone up, and many then also went down, in the years since the World Wide Web has become a common part of modern life.

Some of the Atlanta Child Murders themed websites advance the conspiracy theories, but most actually track the case in a fairly objective manner.

Wayne Williams is also mentioned and featured on several serial killer themed websites.

Since the 2010s, the Atlanta Child Murders case has also become the topic on at least one podcast, which aims to look at the case from a variety of different perspectives.

Along with the true crime books and websites, a few fictional movies were produced that either dealt directly with the case or used it as a plot device.

In 1985, just three years after Williams was convicted of murder and about a year before the *Spin* article, the CBS network aired the miniseries *The Atlanta Child Murders.*

The Atlanta Child Murders was a five-hour, two-part miniseries that aired on CBS in February 1985. Although the series was panned by many critics, it did relatively well ratings wise and boasted of an all-star cast of former and future A-list actors.

Some of the more notable actors who had roles in the series were Jason Robards as one of Williams' attorneys, James Earl Jones as the police chief, Ruby Dee as Wayne Williams' mother, Morgan Freeman, Martin Sheen, Calvin Levels as Wayne Williams, and a young Bill Paxton as officer Campbell.

Although many of the names of the principals involved in the case were retained, a disclaimer was shown before each episode stating that the series was a fictional portrayal of actual events.

The first part of the series is in the format of a basic police procedural show—the Task Force, some of whose names were changed, endure long hours of work, several setbacks, and constant frustration trying to catch the Atlanta Child Killer. The show depicts some of the aspects of the forensic investigation conducted by Larry Peterson and others, which ultimately lead to Williams' arrest.

The trial of Wayne Williams was covered with the implication that Williams received poor representation by his lawyers and the judge was biased against him. Ultimately, *The Atlanta Child Murders* takes the position that Williams was guilty of the crimes for which he was convicted, but leaves open the possibility that other killers, such as the Klan, were responsible for some of the other twenty-six murders.

The Atlanta Child Murders may have partially inspired the publication of the 1986 *Spin* article that advocated the Klan conspiracy angle, which in turn led to a 2000 movie on the Showtime network.

Who Killed Atlanta's Children? is the title of the Showtime movie that starred James Belushi and Gregory Hines as fictional composites of the authors Robert Keating and Barry Michael Cooper, who wrote the 1986 *Spin* article, "A Question of Justice."

The movie follows the two reporters as they dig into the Klan conspiracy theory and reveal what was apparently a conspiracy by the Task Force and the city of Atlanta to cover up a series of racially motivated murders of black boys. The movie plays fast and loose with the facts and gives almost no consideration to the physical evidence that linked Wayne Williams to the victims.

And although Belushi and Hines are both accomplished actors, the scenes are forced and the dialogue is often overly dramatic.

Although *Who Killed Atlanta's Children?* never claimed to be a documentary of the case, like the *Atlanta Child Murders*, it was also panned by critics due to its portrayal of the facts.

The Atlanta Child Murders case has been most widely covered in print. Besides the 1986 *Spin* article, several of books and articles have been published that explore several different facets of this complicated case. Chet Dettlinger, who worked as an investigator with the Task Force, wrote a 1984 book with Jeff Prugh titled *The List* that is highly critical of the official stance on the Atlanta Child Murders case.

The "list" refers to the working list compiled by the Task Force of murdered boys and young men who were believed to have been victims of the Atlanta Child Killer. Although Dettlinger argues that Wayne Williams was more than likely responsible for at least a few of the murders, he is adamant that there were a number of other killers involved. Instead of dredging up the Klan conspiracy theory, Dettlinger explored the possibility of organized pedophile groups operating in the Atlanta area. Dettlinger also wrote that the sexual aspect of the murders was wrongly downplayed by the media and many on the Task Force.

Today, many of the surviving members of the Task Force dispute many of the claims in *The List*.

The Atlanta Child Murders case was next explored in a 1986 non-fiction worked titled *The Moronic Inferno: And Other Visits to America* by British author Martin Amis. The book was a compilation of twenty-six newsworthy events that were covered by Amis, one of which was the Atlanta Child Murders case. For the most part, Amis presented the case as it was shown in the media and avoided any controversial conspiracy theories other than to say that some existed in certain people's minds.

Noted black writer and author of *Native Son*, James Baldwin, penned a story about the Atlanta Child Murders titled *The Evidence of Things Not* Seen that was published in 1984. The book uses a unique "creative non-fiction" style to explore the case through the eyes of one of the victims. Although nothing new is explored in the title, it offers an interesting view on the tragic case.

An academic study of the Atlanta Child Murders case and its wider implications on Atlanta were offered by criminologist Bernard Headley in the 1999 book *The Atlanta Youth Murders and the Politics of Race*. Headley is a PhD in criminology who was in the courtroom every day of Wayne William's trial. Using interviews with those involved, archived news reports, and other primary source material, Headley presents a well-thought title that may be a little too intellectually heavy for those expecting to find another title that deals with some of the conspiracies that keep surrounding this case.

Headley takes the stance that Wayne Williams is responsible for many, if not all of the murders, and although he revisits the evidence that helped put Williams away for life, he focuses his study on the social context of the murders. As the title suggests, Headley examines the role race and politics played in the case and how it may have helped Williams evade capture for so long.

One of the more recent books that concern the case is the 2009 *The Atlanta Child Murders: The Night Stalker* by Jack Mallard.

Mallard was of course the lead prosecutor at Wayne Williams' murder trial and has been quite vocal about his belief that Williams killed most or even all of the victims on the list. In this self-published title, Mallard essentially defends the Task Force's investigation and his prosecution of Williams, pointing out that the physical and circumstantial evidence was overwhelming. Mallard considers the reasons for Dekalb County reopening the case in 2006 and dedicates considerable space to debunk the Klan theory that keeps remerging.

Although *The Atlanta Child Murders: The Night Stalker* has been criticized for its writing style among other things, it has received generally positive reviews.

One of the more interesting aspects of the Atlanta Child Murders case is how interest in it was revived in the Internet era. Numerous websites have popped, many of which focus on the conspiratorial angles, professing to have the final say on the case. In early 2018, the weekly podcast *Atlanta Monster* began airing. The podcast is hosted by documentary filmmaker Payne Lindsey, who aims to consider all aspects of the case from the beginning until the present.

Payne considers all aspects of the case, including the theory that Wayne Williams worked for the CIA, ultimately coming down on the standard idea that Williams committed most of the murders.

CHAPTER 10:
Some Other Notable Black Serial Killers

One of the elements of the Atlanta Child Murders case that perplexed many of Atlanta's black residents was that one of their own was hunting their children. Black youths were killed before and after the two-year murder spree, but most of those murders were either committed by family members of the victims or other youths.

The local, and later national, media further exasperated the problem by promoting the narrative that most, if not all, serial killers were white males. In fairness to the media, as mentioned in the introduction, the serial killer as a criminology phenomenon was new in the late 1970s and early 1980s so their coverage was an evolving process.

Still, the media made many mistakes in their coverage of the Atlanta Child Murders. Instead of doing their due diligence by investigating the facts at hand, many outlets let rumors and conspiracy theories inundate the airwaves.

With that said, most of the members of the Task Force knew that the perpetrator, or perpetrators, of the murders were probably black. The federal and state agents on the Task Force were familiar with Robert Ressler's work and the local and county members knew that it would be nearly impossible for a white killer, or killers, to capture and kill so many black youths from neighborhoods that were almost entirely black.

All of this played to Wayne Williams' advantage as he became perhaps the most notorious black serial killer in American history in terms of kill count and the long-lasting impact he had on the city of Atlanta and even the country.

But Wayne Williams was just one of many notable black serial killers who has launched campaigns of murder across the United States.

Jake Bird (1901-1949)

One of the earliest known and most prolific black serial killers in American history was a mysterious man named Jake Bird. Bird was probably born in 1901 in segregated Louisiana, but little is known about the enigmatic killer's early life. In fact, Bird later claimed that he didn't remember the name of the town where he was raised. When he became a teenager, Bird left Louisiana and embarked on a dual career as a railroad worker and serial killer

Bird spent most of his life traveling across the United States working on the railroads and killing people, becoming not only one of America's first notable black serial killers, but also a successful itinerant serial killer, long before the Interstate Highway system was even an idea.

As Bird traveled from town to town on the tracks, he usually left behind at least one victim. Bird targeted white women who were alone in their homes, robbing, raping, and killing them before making his getaway.

The roaming serial killer was finally captured in the state of Washington in 1947. The evidence against him was immense; he was convicted of murder and executed in 1948.

Before Bird died he put a "hex" on many of the many involved in his case, with several of them supposedly dying early and violent deaths, which added more mystery to an already strange case.

Bird is believed to have murdered at least twelve women and as many as forty-six across the United States. Although Bird's method of operation was fairly standard compared to many of the more well-known serial killers who have come after him, he differed from many, including Wayne Williams, by primarily killing outside of his ethnic group.

Coral Watts was another notorious black serial killer who usually targeted victims outside of his race.

Carl "Coral" Eugene Watts (1953-2007)

Coral Watts, also known as the "Sunday Slasher," may have killed as many as 100 women in the states of Michigan and Texas over an eight-year period. Born and raised in Texas, Watts displayed a propensity for sexual deviancy at an early age by stalking and groping young girls.

Watts' deviancy progressed until he began killing primarily white women in 1974.

He earned his moniker because, like Jake Bird, he would enter his victims' homes when they were alone, but he would usually abduct his victims and then torture and murder them at another location.

Although he rarely raped his victims or did any sort of sex act on his victims that would leave biological evidence, profilers considered his crimes sexual in nature with a racially motivated element. The profilers believed that Watts had a deep-seated hatred for women, particularly white women.

Watts was arrested for attempted murder in Texas in 1982 and given a lengthy prison sentence that was believed would keep him behind bars for the rest of his life, but a loophole in the Texas Department of Corrections "good time" process meant that he was due to be released in 2006.

The extent of Watts' criminal behavior was revealed while he was in prison, which led to an outcry from the public when it became known that a serial killer was possibly being released from an American prison.

In 2004, before Watts was released from prison in Texas, prosecutors in the state of Michigan charged him with murder. Watts was convicted of murder in Michigan and given a life sentence in prison, which is where he died of cancer in 2007.

Watts' M.O. was more similar to Bird's in that he would invade his victims' homes, whereas Wayne Williams would entice his victims to willingly come with him, then he would take them to another location to kill them. For killers such as Watts and Bird, part of the "thrill" of their crimes was derived from invading a home and destroying a person's tranquility and safety.

Wayne Williams got his thrill almost entirely from the kill.

A black serial killer named Lorenzo Gilyard operated in a manner more similar to Williams.

Lorenzo Gilyard

Lorenzo Gilyard may have had a very different background than Wayne Williams, but the two men shared a similar M.O. Gilyard was born in 1950 and spent most of his young life on the streets of Kansas City, Missouri. His father was a convicted sex offender and his siblings were career criminals. Gilyard's mother failed to provide him with the needed moral compass in his father's absence, so he ran the streets learning the tricks of the trade from his family members and other career criminals.

Lorenzo learned how to steal, fight, and sell drugs, but his true criminal calling was sexual violence.

There was no sexual taboo Gilyard wouldn't cross and anyone unlucky to be alone around him became a possible victim. Gilyard served time for raping a thirteen-year-old girl. Despite his chaotic background, Gilyard married and moved around the country working various jobs in the states of California, Nevada, Florida, and Missouri. Like serial killers of every race, Gilyard was able to carefully construct a façade that allowed him to operate with impunity for several years.

It is believed that Gilyard began killing in 1977, taking victims in most of the locations where he lived.

Although Williams and Gilyard had very different backgrounds, the two men collected their victims in a very similar way – they won the confidence of vulnerable individuals and then attacked at opportune moments.

Williams won the confidence of poor young boys and men, while Gilyard focused his violence on prostitutes. Although Gilyard was not as prolific in murder as Williams—he has been credited with thirteen murders—he was able to evade the authorities for a much longer period of time—1977-1993.

Lorenzo Gilyard was found guilty of seven counts of first-degree murder and was sentenced to life without parole in a Missouri prison.

Harrison Graham

Harrison Graham is a hulking, physically intimidating man who grew up on the mean streets of North Philadelphia during the 1970s. To say Graham was not intelligent would certainly be an understatement. From an early age, Graham had problems in school doing the basic work and keeping up with kids his own age.

Today, he would probably be put in remedial classes, but in the 1970s it was sink or swim so Graham sank. Unable to do the work and keep up, Graham dropped out of school at a young age and decided to try his luck on the streets.

Graham then drifted around the streets of Philadelphia committing petty crimes and using his size and strength to extort and rob people.

He also developed a heavy cocaine addiction during the 1980s.

As Graham's life descended into a nearly constant drug binge during the mid-1980s, he began bringing prostitutes to his apartment.

But most of the hookers never left.

Fueled by large amounts of cocaine, Graham would quickly overpower and then rape and strangle, or beat to death, prostitutes whom he brought to his apartment. Instead of disposing of the bodies at another location, Graham kept the corpses in his apartment where he then engaged in necrophilia and other unnatural acts that would have made Jeffery Dahmer proud.

And like Dahmer, Graham's neighbors eventually complained of the putrid smell emanating from his apartment, which led to his arrest for first-degree murder in 1987.

Although initially sentenced to death, Graham won an appeal and is now serving a sentence of life without parole in the Pennsylvania Department of Corrections.

The "Grim Sleeper" Lonnie David Franklin Junior

Franklin Junior grew up on the tough streets of south-central Los Angeles in the 1960s and after a brief and unsuccessful stint in the military during the 1970s, he returned to his old stomping grounds to engage in an activity for which he would be far more successful – serial killing.

After a series of dead-end jobs and a few arrests for petty crimes, Franklin Junior began murdering black prostitutes in 1985 in some of Los Angeles' most crime ridden neighborhoods. Due to the fact that his victims were prostitutes and they were murdered in high crime neighborhoods, it took the police quite some time to realize that the women were victims of a serial killer. Franklin Junior was able to simply hide among the criminal elements in the high-crime, drug-infested neighborhoods of 1980s LA.

As crack began to hit the streets and more and more people walked the streets of south-central Los Angeles in a dazed state, Franklin Junior was able to kill again and again.

Franklin Junior also had the benefit of other serial killers hunting in his territory during the late 1980s, which caused law enforcement officers to confuse him with another serial killer known as the "Southside Slayer." This is actually more common than one may think. For instance, during the 1970s, there were three different "Freeway Killers" operating simultaneously in California who had similar M.O.s and who claimed similar victims, which cause confusion among investigators.

Franklin Junior employed a similar M.O. to Williams' by luring his victims to his home through a ruse, which is where he murdered them. Also, like Williams, Franklin Junior would dump his victims in semi-isolated areas of the city.

But in 1988 Franklin Junior set himself apart from all other known serial killers by going on a nearly fourteen year "cooling off period." The so-called cooling off period is an important aspect of the makeup of a serial killer. It is simply a period of significant time when a serial killer refrains from killing, often after his first or second murder. There is no determinant period of time for a cooling off period, but it is usually weeks or months instead of years.

Law enforcement authorities are confident that Franklin Junior didn't kill anyone from 1988 until 2002, which is how he earned his nickname the "Grim Sleeper."

By the time Franklin Junior was finally arrested in 2010, he may have murdered up to twenty-five people, all but one of them women.

The Grim Sleeper was found guilty of first-degree murder in a Los Angeles County courtroom and sentenced to death in 2016.

The "Southside Slayer" Chester Dewayne Turner

Many Los Angeles Police Department and Los Angeles Sherriff's Department investigators believed that the Grim Sleeper was the South Side Slayer because both men hunted in the same neighborhoods and Turner became active when Franklin Junior went on his extra-long cooling off period.

Turner moved to Los Angeles with his mother when he was a boy during the 1970s, but he soon learned that the streets weren't paved in gold. He struggled to make a living doing low-paying manual labor and cooking jobs, often living in homeless shelters and on the streets.

Although Turner learned that life could be tough in the City of Angles, he also found out that there were no shortage of victims to satiate his sick desires.

Turner was arrested several times and did time in prison during the 1980s and 1990s for a host of crimes ranging from theft to assault and rape.

He began killing women in 1988, usually prostitutes, in a small area of south-central Los Angeles, rarely leaving a four-block corridor. Most serial killers are known to operate in a comfort zone, but the Southside Slayer took the idea to another level. Serial killers do this because they know the routines of potential victims, and the police, in comfort zones, as well as good dump sites.

Unlike Franklin Junior, whose geographic kill zone he overlapped with, Turner strangled most of his victims after raping them. He was also much more brazen, usually killing the women on the streets.

The Southside Slayer was convicted of murder and sentenced to death in 2007 and now sits on California's death row. He is believed to have killed at least fifteen women from 1988 to 1998.

Maury Travis (1965-2002), the Videotape Killer

Many notable criminals have come from the streets of St. Louis, Missouri over the years, but few have been as deadly as Maury Travis. Like most serial killers, Travis was relatively unassuming and although not particularly bright or good-looking, he did have a certain amount of charisma.

Travis was able to move back and forth from the criminal underworld of drugs and prostitutes to a politer society as he worked normal jobs. Despite his often calm exterior, Travis had a rage burning inside him that could not be quenched.

He landed in state prison in Missouri during the 1990s for a violent crime and when he was released he appeared to be walking the straight and narrow. He worked as a waiter in a St. Louis restaurant where all of his co-workers described him as polite and helpful and his regular customers thought he was fairly charming.

But when Travis punched out from his job serving the hungry citizens of St. Louis, he roamed the city's poorest neighborhoods looking for murder victims.

Travis directed his fury at some of society's most vulnerable people—prostitutes. From the late 1990s until the early 2000s, Travis raped and murdered up to seventeen prostitutes, dumping their bodies in remote locations around the St. Louis metropolitan area. It was a while before law enforcement even knew they had a serial killer on their hands and when they discover a serial killer was murdering prostitutes in St. Louis they had no idea who he was.

But then Travis made a costly mistake.

In late 2001, full of arrogance like most serial killers, Travis mailed a taunting letter to a journalist at *The St. Louis-Post Dispatch*. In the letter, the killer boasted about his killing prowess and included a map that led to the body of his seventh victim.

The police were able to locate the website where the map was downloaded from and narrowed down the time when it was printed. They finally were able to get the IP address of Travis' computer.

After Travis was arrested, the police found a secret torture chamber in his basement and several videotapes of him torturing and murdering prostitutes.

While Travis was awaiting trial on first-degree murder charges in the St. Louis County Jail, he hanged himself, thereby closing the case but leaving some unanswered questions.

Wayne Williams Takes His Place among His Peers

In many ways, Wayne Williams was similar to not just these other notorious black serial killers, but all serial killers in general. Although Williams was not known to have displayed any of the traits of the Macdonald Triad – excessive bedwetting after age five, pyromania, and cruelty to animals – he did exhibit other behaviors from an early age that were common to many other serial killers.

Williams was a consummate loner, who had many acquittances and business associates but very few if any close friends, male or female.

Wayne Williams was also plagued by delusions of grandeur. He has been described by many experts as a pathological liar who lives in a fantasy world. As will be seen, many of Williams' fantasies involved him "cleansing the world" of undesirables.

Although at first glance it may not seem so, Wayne Williams truly fits the profile of a classic serial killer.

There was just that final thread keeping Williams from crossing the line from standard sociopath to serial killer. It will probably never be known if something "triggered" Williams into cutting that thread and crossing the line, or if his murderous impulses festered deep within his essence since childhood until he could no longer contain them.

In the summer of 1979, Wayne Williams was getting ready to show the world what he was all about.

Conclusion

The Atlanta Child Murders case was like no other in American history and in many ways would make a perfect fictional story.

But unfortunately, the Atlanta Child Murders were all too real.

During a nearly two-year period, from the summer of 1979 until May 1981, twenty-eight black children and young black adults disappeared from the streets of Atlanta only to turn up later in vacant lots and rivers around the metropolitan area. The crimes were senseless, brutal crimes shocked the residents of the city and as the murders continued, they shocked people around the world.

The media played a major role in the Atlanta Child Murders case as it followed the killings in "real time," updating the public on the number killed and what, if anything, law enforcement was doing to stop the murders.

As the body count increased, it became clear to Atlantans that young blacks, especially boys, were the sole targets of the killer. The black community panicked and rumors began to spread that the murders were all part of an elaborate hate crime campaign, possibly being conducted by members of the Ku Klux Klan.

Although Atlanta's city government and police force were predominantly black at that time, the old ghosts of the south continued to haunt the city, which gave life to the Klan conspiracy theories.

Finally, due to the combined pressure from the media and some of the victims' families, a Task Force was created from officers in local, county, state, and federal law enforcement agencies to catch the killer or killers.

The idea of hunting a serial killer was new to the media and public and even law enforcement for the most part since the term was only first coined about five years before the Atlanta Child Murders case.

As Wayne Williams hunted and murdered black children and young black males on the streets of Atlanta, the Task Force was hot on his tail using two new criminology methods that would eventually take him down.

The first method the Task Force used was profiling.

The idea of "profiling" an unknown offender was new in the late 1970s as it had only been introduced to criminal investigations in the mid-1970s by FBI agent Robert Ressler and the FBI's Behavioral Science Unit. Profilers working with the Task Force accurately predicted that the offender would be a loner who was employed or worked nights and would probably have no significant other. The profilers also determined that the crimes were probably sexual in nature and that most importantly the killer was black.

Wayne Williams fit the profile to a tee.

The profilers were also instrumental in Williams' eventual capture.

After closely examining the killer's pattern of dumping his victims, the profilers recommended to Task Force that all river bridges and vacant lots in the Atlanta be closely watched.

The profilers were right once again.

The other major new law enforcement technique that played a central role in the Atlanta Child murders case was fiber evidence.

Although the use of carpet and rug fiber evidence had been used in previous cases, it was still a fairly new technique when the Task Force used it in their investigation. After Wayne Williams was stopped on the bridge, it was only a matter of time before the investigators could match fibers found on some of the victims to rugs and carpets from Williams' home and car.

The combination of circumstantial evidence and physical evidence in the form of fibers and hairs was just too much for Wayne Williams to overcome at trial. He was found guilty of two murders by a jury of his peers and sentenced to life in prison.

In the years since Williams' convictions, interest in the Atlanta Child Murders case has ebbed and flowed. Whenever Williams' attempts a new appeal, the case temporarily makes it into the headlines and then quickly recedes from it when the appeal is denied.

Some of the bizarre theories continue to persist, thanks in large part now to the Internet, but most involved, including the victims' families, believe that Wayne Williams is right where he belongs.

Few people doubt that Wayne Williams is a killer, or even a serial killer, but the exact number of victims he claimed is in dispute and may never be known.

Perhaps once Williams realizes that he will never leave prison, his ego will get the better of him and he'll confess to more of the murders. Until that time, it is anyone's guess just how many of Atlanta's children Wayne Williams murdered during that two-year span in the late 1970s and early 1980s.

More books by Jack Rosewood

Few serial killers in history have garnered as much attention as Jeffrey Lionel Dahmer. Although Dahmer killed seventeen young men and boys, it was not so much the number of people he killed that makes him stand out among famous serial killers, but more so the acts of depravity that he committed on the corpses of his victims. In this true crime story you will read how Dahmer transitioned from a loner to serial killer, committing numerous unnatural acts along the way such as necrophilia and cannibalism. Following in the macabre tradition of another infamous Wisconsin serial killer—Ed Gein—Jeffrey Dahmer terrorized Milwaukee for most of the 1980s until he was finally captured in 1991.

Perhaps one of the most frightening aspects of Jeffrey Dahmer's serial killer career was how easy he was able to lure his victims into his trap. Dahmer possessed above average intellect, was conventionally good looking, and usually had a calm demeanor that could disarm even the most paranoid of people. Because of these traits, Dahmer was able to evade justice numerous times, which allowed him to keep killing. Truly, Dahmer was able to fool his family, the police, his neighbors, and even the judicial system into believing that he was not a threat; but during the entire time his kill count increased and the body parts of his victims began to pile up around his apartment.

Open the pages of this book to read a story that is among the most disturbing of all true crime serial killers. You will follow the course of Dahmer's life from an alcoholic outcast in high school to a vicious predator who stalked the streets of Milwaukee. Finally, you will read about Dahmer's trial, his jail house murder, and the impact that his many crimes had on Milwaukee.

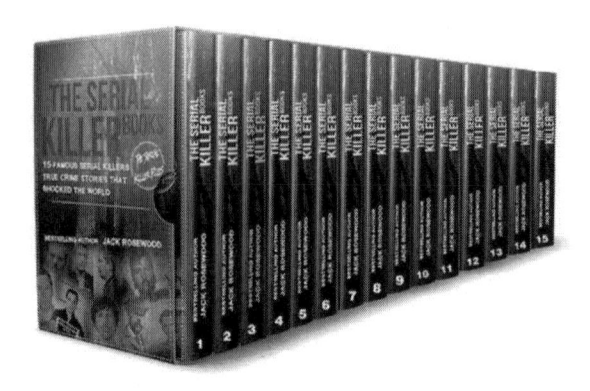

There are reasons why some of the most famous serial killers in the world have names that stick in our memories, send shivers up our spines, make us double-check to make sure the doors are locked at night, and maybe peek under the bed to be sure nothing is lurking there before we turn off the lights.

These are monsters who are real, whose crimes are so reprehensible, so horrific, that they become seared in our memories.

For this true crime anthology, we've combed the serial killer files to give you a closer, more intimate look at some of the worst of the worst from the world of serial killer, combining multiple stories into one perfect late-night read that's just the thing to keep you up at night, unable to stop turning the pages.

For those who love criminology, who can't put down the latest true crime stories, this collection of stories rivals the best serial killer books, and give you deeper insight into killers ranging from the charismatic, cunning Ted Bundy to the long-abused Aileen Wuornos, whose unimaginable troubles finally came to a very violent head.

This diverse collection of serial killer stories, culled from the annals of history, is an ideal choice for the true crime buff who wonders why the monsters of our imaginations came to life and walked the streets, lurking in dark corners to wait for their next victim.

GET THESE BOOKS FOR FREE

Go to www.jackrosewood.com/free

and get these E-Books for free!

A Note From The Author

Hello, this is Jack Rosewood. Thank you for reading this book. I hope you enjoyed the read. If you did, I'd appreciate if you would take a few moments to **post a review on Amazon.**

I would also love if you'd sign up to my newsletter to receive updates on new releases, promotions and a FREE copy of my Herbert Mullin E-Book, www.JackRosewood.com

Thanks again for reading this book, make sure to follow me on Facebook.

Best Regards

Jack Rosewood

Printed in Great Britain
by Amazon